P9-DCT-384

As a lifelong advocate for the humane treatment of animals—and the founder/owner of A Place To Bark, a no-kill, foster and adoption rescue nonprofit—I wholeheartedly support the mission and spirit of B. J. Taylor and her CHARLIE BEAR.

I have *known* all types of pets; yet the headstrong ones like Charlie, which B. J. depicts so accurately and engagingly, have always seemed to capture my heart. And the fact that Charlie inspires so much love—and ultimately turns the tables and rescues "his" humans!—makes this book a must-read for dog lovers across the globe!

Bernie Berlin, Founder, A Place To Bark

"An endearingly straightforward tale of a dog and the love he inspires."

Ptolemy Tompkins, author of *The Divine Life of Animals*
Contributing Editor, *Guideposts*
Senior Contributing Editor, *Angels on Earth*

Charlie Bear

*What a Headstrong Rescue Dog Taught Me
about Life, Love, and Second Chances*

B. J. Taylor

Guideposts
New York

ISBN: 978-1-4624-0117-8 (e)
ISBN: 978-1-4624-0116-1 (sc)

Library of Congress Control Number: 2012936432

Inspiring Voices books may be ordered through booksellers or by contacting:

Inspiring Voices
1663 Liberty Drive
Bloomington, IN 47403
www.inspiringvoices.com
1-(866) 697-5313

Cover by Müllerhaus

Interior photographs by Ryoko Matsui/Cheryl Maneff.

Printed in the United States of America

Inspiring Voices rev. date: 4/09/2012

PROLOGUE

THANKSGIVING RUSHES BY IN a frenzy of too much turkey, stuffing, and cream-topped pie. Stores decked out in holiday green and red usher in the Christmas season. Salvation Army Santa Clauses stand outside and ring their bells, while carols blare from car radios, televisions, and overhead speakers at the mall.

We dig out all the decorations for the house and hang the oversized, paw-shaped stocking with the embroidered white "Rex" over the fireplace.

"We need a stocking for Charlie Bear," Roger reminds me.

"It's your first Christmas with us, cute face." I bend over to pet him. He wiggles, shakes, and then rolls over onto his back. "Huh, look at that." I reach out and rub his tummy.

"Good boy, Charlie," Roger says.

I buy a medium-sized red stocking and write the name Charlie in white Elmer's Glue across the top. Holding the stocking over a newspaper, I shake silver glitter over the cursive writing. When it's dry, I hang Charlie's next to Rex's and admire them.

The little and the big. Size is only one of the differences between them.

On New Year's Day last year, when I packed the boxes of decorations, I put our cats' tiny, four-inch stockings right on top. I unfold the tissue paper now, finger the soft red felt, and trace their names, Diamond and Red, in silver glitter. I rewrap the stockings in tissue, leave them nestled together, and place them back in the box.

On my way to the garage with the now almost-empty carton, I glance at the silver-framed photographs on a small table in the family room. There's one of Diamond and Red, curled together in the same basket we put outside for a feral cat when she was about to give birth. When she no longer needed it, I brought the wicker basket into the house and lined it with a clean, large, soft towel. Diamond and Red loved the size; it was perfect for them to nestle together.

Red was the more social of the two cats, and family and friends knew him well. Stretched out in a beam of sunlight or lying on the stairs, he was always around.

No one ever saw Diamond. When the doorbell rang or a knock startled her, her eyes grew wide, and she'd turn from wherever she was and dash up the stairs to hide. Her favorite place to cower was in my closet, and I left one of the doors open so she could go inside anytime she wanted to. It was her refuge. If I ever had to look for her, that's where she'd be—tucked way in the corner underneath my clothes.

After Diamond had her stroke and left us, more than a week passed before I could close my closet doors all the way. The first time I did, it felt final and wrong. We missed her immensely.

CHAPTER ONE

October 2010

"Hon, do you think the day will come when we don't have any pets?" I look at my husband. His hand caresses the top of our golden Lab's head.

"I don't think so," Roger answers.

Grief etches his face; his puffy red eyes match mine.

"It's so hard to lose them." I dab at my eyes with the ever-ready Kleenex I keep in my hand lately.

"I know. It's because we love them so much."

Roger and I first met in 1988. I lived in Wisconsin at the time, and he lived in California. Roger had a thriving career selling products to landscapers, and I worked as an administrative assistant. It's not easy to get to know someone from afar, so two years later, I moved to California. We married in 1994 and settled in Southern California, where we now work together in a small business selling landscape products.

One of the things that attracted me to Roger was his deep love for animals. It mirrored my own. We had both grown up with dogs and cats, and right after marrying, we welcomed both into our home.

Now, we were recovering from losing Red, our fifteen-and-a-half-year-old marmalade cat. Red was a love bug. He'd snuggle next to me and rub his head all over my hair after I'd had a weave and a shampoo. He'd meow loudly, sit on the kitchen counter, and wait stoically for his insulin shots. Diagnosed with diabetes when he was ten, he needed insulin and a special diabetic-management cat food. We received a crash course in the many types of syringes and learned that short, ultrafine were best for Red.

After overcoming my queasiness about needles, and seeing that the short ones weren't so menacing, it became second nature for me to give him his insulin shot twice a day. We structured our lives around the morning dosage, which we gave him when we woke up. And we were sure to be home twelve hours later when he needed his nighttime dosage. Red took each shot with courage; he seemed to know the insulin made him feel better. And for the first four and a half years, it did. Then he took a turn for the worse.

"What should I do with the insulin?" It isn't a question—more of a plea.

The refrigerator door stands open, and in my hand sits the tiny glass bottle with the orange cap. We keep it in the small cardboard carton it comes in, so it doesn't get jostled around or broken, like the one time it slipped from my fingers and shattered on the kitchen floor. After an emergency trip to the pharmacy, a replacement had been procured. Not wanting to part with it for some sentimental reason, I tuck the bottle into the back of the pull-out drawer and shut the refrigerator door.

"And what about the syringes?" Again, this is only a muffled, half-whispered question. Buying needles at the drugstore raised an eyebrow or two, especially with a new pharmacist. "Who is this for?" he'd inevitably ask. And once again, I'd have to explain that Red Taylor was our cat. Invariably, he'd call the vet's office for confirmation. I open the box of syringes. It's almost full.

Not expecting a response from my husband, I put the box of needles aside and join him in the family room, taking my usual spot on the sofa across from him. Red always jumped up next to me. Not anymore.

That's when all the heartache floods back of that difficult decision we had to make to help him over the rainbow bridge into heaven. It was only a few days ago, but I know I'll never forget the date, October 1, when I held him in my arms and caressed his sweet face as the vet administered the shot to put him to sleep.

Losing Red is tough, but it's even tougher because Diamond had a stroke and died in her sleep only eight months before. She'd been fifteen and a half too. Red had missed Diamond, his inseparable, best buddy, as much as we did. I missed Diamond's sweet face, Red's insistent meows, and the love they both gave to Roger and me.

I look at Rex, our beautiful golden Lab. Floppy, cocoa-colored ears, much darker than the rest of him, stand out against his short-haired, caramel coat. Splotches of sunshine adorn his sides. He isn't a lap dog; he's way too big. But I often sit on the floor and hold him halfway on my lap. He grew from a capricious, gangly pup into a strong, mature, confident dog.

Wherever I go, he follows. His eyes are constantly on me, and he remains as near to me as he can get. A while ago, I placed a carpet runner on the floor at the end of the sofa for Rex. He stretches his body out on that carpet each night.

He's the only pet left in the house, except for Smokey, a partly feral outdoor cat. I'll tell you more about him later.

A few days later, Roger mentions our son Tim, who often visits with his two Yorkies. Wonderful little playthings, they jump around and make us laugh. They're completely different from Rex, who is slowing down considerably at age ten.

"Let's get a dog like those," Roger says.

"Now? Don't you think we'd be making a decision on the rebound, wanting another pet simply because we're hurting?"

"No, I don't think so."

"Maybe we should wait a while." I lock eyes with him. The grief from losing Red is piercing. Do I really want to turn over my heart to another pet, only to have it get broken again?

"Let's just look, okay? We don't have to decide right away."

"Yeah, but I know you. If you start looking, you'll fall for one, and then we'll have another pet in the house."

"So, what's wrong with that?"

I can't tell him I don't want any more heartbreak. Rex pushes his wet nose into my hand. My eyes mist up just thinking about it. Though I miss our cats immensely, Rex is still here, and he is definitely enough for me.

Then I look at my sweet husband. He misses Red's meows for breakfast and dinner, his purrs as he lay down for his insulin shots, his meows of pleasure when Roger opened the slider to give Red a breeze while he was sunning himself.

"Let's get one of those Yorkies," Roger says.

Once he has his mind made up, there's no arguing with him. And besides, he's been going through a challenge of his own. Two months ago, he quit smoking, and it hasn't been easy for him. If he wants a Yorkie, I'll go along with it. I admit I do miss having a small, furry friend in the house, and there are so many dogs that need homes.

I try to swallow my fear of more heartache as well as my unfounded fear of having a tiny dog. They look so fragile. The smallest dog I've ever had was a beagle/Chihuahua mix when I was a teenager. At twenty-two pounds, I could pick Bogie up, carry him around, and snuggle in bed with him at night.

"They're cute," I tell Roger, "but how about one slightly bigger?"

"I want a little one," he retorts.

Most of the dogs and cats Roger and I have welcomed into our lives have come from a visit to a shelter or through a sign posted at a vet's office. But our son Craig adopted a beautiful, sweet, one-and-a-half-year-old Rottweiler from an online rescue service. The dog had been abandoned and was being fostered in a nearby town. He was a perfect match for our son.

I google the words "adoption rescue site," click on the first one, type in "Yorkie," and list our parameters. Roger wants a young dog, while I lobby for an older one that needs a home. We agree on an age older than a puppy. The gender doesn't matter.

Up pops page after page of tiny Yorkies, some with pink bows on their heads, others with little sweaters on, some standing proud and boasting a little-dog attitude, and others cowering from the camera, shy and demure. How can we choose? What makes a dog right for us? Or what makes us right for the dog?

I click over to individual bios. "Okay, I found some. They're all around six pounds or so. I'll print pictures for you."

The printer chugs and spits out one and then two, three, and four different photos with bios and adoption information. *Are we doing the right thing?* While Roger sometimes jumps in with both feet, I'm the one who thinks long and hard and weighs all the pros and cons, often taking forever to make a decision. He sees the big picture; I have a hard time looking past the first detail. I focus on the extra work of another pet and the resulting heartbreak. He sees the love, companionship, and joy another pet will bring to our lives.

I love and trust Roger, and if he wants a tiny Yorkie, then that's what we'll get.

While waiting for the printing to finish, I scroll to the end of the page of the online site and see a notation. "Other dogs you might be interested in." A few photographs come up. The very first one shows a dog named Charlie Bear. *What a face,* I think instantly. *And look at the tilt of his head.* His breed is listed as shih tzu/terrier mix; his size is small, under twenty-five pounds. And his color says gray/silver/salt-and-pepper with white. His sex is male, and he is young.

Even though his adorable features catch my attention, it's the line right under his name that tugs at my heart. "I need a home and someone to love me." *How could someone not love this dog?* I keep reading and learn the dog has "issues." His bio goes on to say: "When he settles into his daily routine and feels secure and relaxed, he turns into a Charlie Bear—the sweetest, most affectionate, and cuddliest teddy bear."

Without thinking twice, I print his info and stick it at the bottom of the stack I printed for Roger. The pictures of the little Yorkies are awesomely cute, but this guy—well, there's just something about him.

Roger looks at the photographs and the bios. I try not to watch him, but I steal glances in his direction. He flips through the first two quite fast and reads a bit on the rest. Finally, he's done.

He raises his hand in the air, holding a set of papers. "This is the one."

The papers aren't turned toward me, and I can't see the photograph. Did he choose the little female Yorkie, or maybe the male? I walk over to him.

In his hand is Charlie Bear's info.

"You like this one?"

"I do," Roger replies.

A little shocked that we both like the same dog, and not quite believing it could be true, I admonish myself for being surprised. *Aren't we often like that?* We choose something individually, and then we come together to share our opinions, only to discover we feel the same way. A color choice on carpet? The granite for the kitchen countertop? We always agree. It has happened more than a dozen times during our seventeen-year marriage.

I have to point out what we both already know though. "But he has a bunch of issues."

Charlie Bear's bio states he's about fourteen months old and weighs almost twenty pounds. It also says he spent his formative puppy months fending for himself on the streets with an owner who didn't care for him. As a result, he developed some "issues."

There in bolded typeface, so anyone reading about this dog won't miss it, it states: "His issues include resource guarding, being sensitive to touch and throwing tantrums caused by frustration." Even though the typeface is no longer bold, the next words carry weight just the same. "He chases his tail aggressively when he is nervous, overly excited, or unable to do what he wants to do."

I wonder if this dog has too many problems. *Do we want a dog like that?* I had a dog once—part-shepherd and part-Lab—that didn't like men's work boots, but that's minor compared to this dog's issues.

"Not liking to be touched worries me, Roger. Don't we want a dog we can hold and love?"

"Let's meet him and then decide."

I sit down. My heart is having a boxing match with my head. As soon as I see Charlie's picture, I'm smitten, and it looks like Roger is too. But are we ready for a young whippersnapper of a dog again, let alone one with so many issues?

His photo sits in front of me.

"It's a darn good thing he's cute," I mumble.

Chapter Two

THE ONLINE APPLICATION FORM asks a number of questions. When Craig adopted, he had three pages to fill out. We find ourselves doing the same thing, answering questions about pets we've had before, if we own or rent our home, if the yard is completely fenced, if we know who will care for our pet when we go away, and if we are willing to be responsible for a dog for the next ten to fifteen years. They also query us if we have pets now and what our plans are for helping the new dog adjust to the household. The thoroughness of the application shows me they care.

Roger and I have had all kinds of dogs over the years, from mixed breeds to purebreds, from small Bogie to a large Samoyed named Casper, and everything in between. As a puppy, Rex was rescued from a cage in a pet store and has always been the only dog in the house, having to share only with cats. I don't mind that, especially because Rex has tons of fun when he plays with his friends.

What will Rex think of a new dog joining our domain, sharing his space? Is it fair to him to add another dog to the household at his age?

As we answer all the questions on the form, a niggling sense of apprehension fills me. We note our current dog situation, our work situation (I go to the office in the afternoons, while Roger is out all day making sales calls), and the fact that our yard has a brick wall all the way around for security.

I speculate on whether we'll be considered suitable "parents" for a dog looking for adoption. This reminds me of when I want to win a door prize. I buy the tickets, deposit them into the drawing basket, and then hope, pray, and wish my ticket will be the winner.

Roger wants this dog, and I want him because Roger does. This dog must have other people interested in him. How could he not? He's over-the-top cute.

I check my e-mail thirty times that day. Finally, we get a message that it appears we'll be a good home for Charlie Bear *if* he adjusts well. He has those issues, his rescuer points out, and she's looking for a set of particularly dog-savvy people who can handle his needs. She adds he'll be on a two-week probationary tryout period. I print the message and bring it to Roger.

Roger is in his recliner, watching a hockey game on television, when I walk into the room. I hand him the piece of paper, and he reaches to his side table and grabs his reading glasses.

"What do you think?" I ask after Roger scans the e-mail.

"Let's meet him."

"But we're going away for three days next week."

"Set it up for Saturday when we come home, early in the afternoon. Have her bring Charlie Bear here." He reclines his chair and places his arms behind his head. He's wearing a light gray T-shirt, a pair of comfortable jersey pants and his favorite pair of brown corduroy slippers.

"But they say a dog in a foster home always shows better where he is," I add. "He's more comfortable there."

"I understand that, but I want to meet him here, on our turf. We want to see how he gets along with Rex, right?"

"You're right. But what if she won't bring him here? It's a long way for her to come."

"Burbank is only fifty miles away," Roger says.

"That'll take an hour or more, depending on traffic."

"All you can do is ask."

With trepidation, I e-mail back and ask her to come on Saturday or Sunday of the following weekend. Nervous that both Charlie Bear's rescuer and his foster mom will deny the request, and even if he'll still be available by then, I try to prepare for disappointment. I tell myself if this one doesn't work out, we can look for another. There are so many that need homes—hundreds in our area, thousands all over the state.

But there's something about this dog. I don't want to return to the online site and search through more photos and bios. When I shop, it's natural for me to check all the stores in the mall even if I've already found a great dress in the first store I walk into. I'm the kind of person who likes to confirm there isn't anything better out there.

Not this time.

But that's my emotional side, my gut-intuition side. Then there's my practical side; the one that says *maybe this isn't meant to be*. This dog has a lot of problems to overcome, and if it doesn't work out, maybe it's for the best.

I try to remain neutral, but I still look at his picture a hundred times.

Then I look at Rex. He's enough.

But why can't I get this dog out of my mind?

The e-mail comes the next day. "Yes," it reads, "we can bring him to your house a week from Saturday."

I'm relieved, for Roger's sake, and I'm curious and can't wait to meet him. We agree on one o'clock that Saturday afternoon.

In the meantime, we have a trip to take.

CHAPTER THREE

MONTHS AGO, ROGER ASKED what I want for my birthday. I'm a simple girl and have pretty much everything I need, but there is one thing I'd like. I'd like to see Terry Fator's show at the Mirage in Las Vegas. He has his own theater, and since winning *America's Got Talent*, he has added new puppets and new routines. Roger and I watched each week, and each week we fell further in love with Terry Fator and his engaging act. His singing and ventriloquism are phenomenal, and the puppets are captivating.

"All I want is tickets to see him perform live," I tell Roger.

"Then that's what we'll do. I'll take you to the Mirage to see his show."

"Should we drive or fly?" I ask Roger.

"Let's drive. It'll be a nice road trip, don't you think?"

"Okay." We've done the three hundred-mile trip before, driving to Las Vegas in under five and a half hours.

"Find out if he's playing around your birthday, and get us good seats."

The map of the theater shows a large, yet intimate, setting, and I find seats eight rows up on the right-hand side of the stage. Terry holds the puppets in his right hand when he's on stage, so the puppets will face the right-hand side of the theater; we'll be well-positioned to see the puppets' expressive movements. I've been excited for weeks to see him perform.

But now I have second thoughts.

"Maybe we should cancel our trip," I tell Roger.

"Why would we do that? Haven't you been waiting for this?"

"Yes, I have, and I do want to see him, but there's this dog…" I trail off and run a hand through my hair.

"Charlie Bear? We're going to see him the day we get back."

"But what if they give him to someone else before that?" I bite down on my lower lip. I don't want to invest my heart in a new dog, but here I am already feeling a tug toward one I haven't even met.

"They're not going to give him to someone else. They said they like us, and if it all works out, he'll be ours." Roger looks straight at me.

"Maybe we should see him before we go," I counter.

"It's only a week. Wouldn't it be better to wait until we get back so, if it all works out, we can accept him that same day?"

"Yes, but—"

"But nothing," Roger says kindly. "It'll be okay. You'll see. We'll have a good time and come back and meet the dog." He laughs and hugs me.

We already paid for the tickets and the hotel.

"Okay, we'll go." I hug him.

The night we arrive, we check into our hotel and go for a walk. The sparkling lights and booming music from the fountains at the Bellagio draw us in. I love the dancing waters and stand there mesmerized. The water reaches for the heavens and then falls in a rush into the pool below. As the music becomes intense, the water twirls, shoots skyward, and falls with a *whoosh*. My tears fall with it.

"Why are you crying?" Roger asks as he pulls me close. "You like this."

"I do, but I don't know," is all I can manage as we watch the rest of the water show play out.

I wipe my eyes and sniff. "I'm okay. Missing Red, I guess."

"I miss him too," Roger answers.

"It was tough saying good-bye." I look into Roger's eyes, and he puts his strong arms around me.

We walk down the strip; both sides of the street boast towering, monstrous resorts that glitter with blinking lights and garish marquees flashing information faster than one can read it. "Ninety-nine-cent shrimp cocktails," advertises one. "The best steakhouse in town," says another.

Our hotel is half a block off the strip. The doorman pulls open the heavy entry door. "Welcome back," he states as we pass through.

The lobby is spacious and inviting. We walk to the bank of elevators, ride up to the tenth floor, and phone our pet's caretaker, Emily. It's her first time taking care of our household without Red, and I can hear the sadness in her voice when I talk to her. Red adored her. She has given him many shots over the years and lovingly cared for all of our other pets.

She tells me Rex is delighted to see her. She put him to bed in his room, and all is well.

"We'll be home Saturday by noon. Get Rex up in the morning and put him outside with the garage side door open, so he can rest on his blankets."

I can count on Emily to take good care of him for the two nights we'll be gone.

The next evening we dress up a bit for our night out. I pull on a pair of black slacks, a red blouse, and a wrap-around, cable-knit, white sweater. Never one to fuss in the fashion department—unless it's a big event, such as a wedding—I stick to clothes that mix and match well. I add a pair of black heels, simple red earrings, and I'm ready to go.

Roger takes the opportunity to wear his nice pair of chocolate-colored corduroy slacks, which he belts at the waist over a checkered shirt and a sleeveless vest.

"You look great," I comment.

"So do you," he responds.

Even with heels, at five feet six inches, I'm a lot shorter than my six-foot one-inch husband. It was one of the many things that drew me to him when we fell in love.

We arrive early at the Mirage and walk the long way to the Terry Fator Theatre. The marquis exclaims, "World Class Impersonator, Comedian, Singer, and Ventriloquist," and it's all true. We sink into our seats, which are so close to the stage we can see the hair on the puppets' heads and every wink and smile from Terry as he does one shtick after another.

Man, what a show he puts on. We laugh with such intensity my belly hurts. The crowd around us claps with enthusiasm and we join in for a standing ovation at the end.

"That was fantastic," I tell Roger as we walk out of the theater.

"One of the best shows I've ever seen."

"Don't you love his new puppet? What's she called—Diva something?"

"And the Neighbor is new too."

"Thanks for the great birthday present." I squeeze Roger tight.

"You're welcome. But there's still more to come."

"What?" I jump out in front of him and peer into his eyes.

"A new dog," he adds.

I grin. "Maybe."

He takes my hand and we walk to the car. "We'll be home tomorrow. Are you excited about meeting him?"

"Yes. You?"

"Yup."

We pull into the driveway at eleven the next morning. Rex greets us with a deep, throaty bark—his usual method of saying hello—and a full-body wiggle.

"You got to see Emily, Rex. Were you a good boy?" I smooth the top of his head and rub behind his ears. "You're a very good boy."

He dashes over to his toys, grabs a squishy brown bear, and brings it over to me. "We missed you, Rex." I hug him tight.

When I correspond with Charlie Bear's rescuer and foster mom, I ask if there is anything in particular I should do to make the meeting with Rex any easier.

"I'm not sure," Sara, his foster mom, replies. "I'll hold Charlie up high and away from Rex when we first arrive."

Since Charlie has been living in a foster home with a large dog and a smaller dog, he's used to other dogs. But still, with Charlie's issues, I'm a little nervous about how we'll all get along. I decide to take Rex for a walk right after lunch, hoping to tire him out a bit so he'll be less likely to be rambunctious. At his age, he doesn't have a lot of rambunctiousness in him, but I'm hoping for a smooth meeting.

The doorbell rings right at one o'clock. I take a deep breath and go to the door.

CHAPTER FOUR

THE FIRST THING I observe when I open the door is that Charlie Bear is even more adorable than his photographs. His mostly gray body—some light, some dark—is tinged with brown in a few places. What stands out is the shockingly white and furry cowlick I first notice on top of his head. My eyes then move to the front of his face, where the white surrounds his entire nose and mouth. The whiteness continues, as if he threw on a tuxedo bib, down his chest and legs. He looks like he pulled on four socks of curly white fur up over his paws. The tip of his tail, with a splash of white, is the final exclamation point.

His foster mom holds him in her arms.

"Let's let Rex sniff him before I put him down," Sara says.

Rex lopes to the front door and skids to a stop. His tail wags a greeting, and he sniffs Charlie Bear. Then, when I call him to the screen door, he trots over, ready to go play in the yard.

"Do you want to come into the yard and put him down?" I ask.

"Great, we'll let them get used to each other out there."

Sara carries Charlie Bear outside. Ryo, his rescuer, is right behind. We all introduce ourselves, and Roger sits on one of the lawn chairs. Sara sets Charlie Bear on the concrete patio, and he begins to sniff the yard, the pots of flowers, and the grassy area off to one side. Rex runs around the end of the house and comes toward us with his scrap of a blanket.

"Look at him; he's got his blankie," Ryo exclaims.

"He's had that thing since puppyhood," I say. "It's really chewed up and one-tenth the size it used to be, but he loves it."

Rex doesn't pay much attention to the new dog. We socialized Rex as a youngster with dogs big and small, yet I watch him closely here. He shakes his blanket from left to right. He can be aggressive if a dog tries to mount him or gets up in his face somehow. Though Rex has never chomped down on anything (his blanket being the exception), little Charlie Bear could be mincemeat in Rex's strong, powerful jaws.

"I don't mean to be pessimistic," Sara offers, "but you should know Charlie will most likely act out the first week he's with you. He guards his food and toys obsessively, and he'll growl and snap if you try to take them away."

I stand to the side, near Rex, and look at this new little dog. I understand he's proven himself to be quite bullheaded, but I wonder how such a cutie can be so much trouble.

"I'm only being super careful," Sara continues. "His tantrums may be minimal, but he does act out whenever he's under any kind of stress."

"He still runs back and forth in the yard, doesn't he?" Ryo asks Sara.

"Yes, he still does that incessantly, and he barks a lot too, at anything and everything—other dogs he hears over the fence, the garbage collectors, the mailman, you name it."

It's clear both Ryo and Sara have misgivings about his adoptability and are checking us out as much as we're checking out Charlie Bear. Now Sara speaks freely.

"We need a couple who can be firm with this dog, and yet be loving as well." Sara looks from Roger to me.

Ryo continues, "We're looking for savvy adopters who are committed to putting in the time required to keep rehabilitating him. He needs to continue to have his training reinforced. Sara has worked hard to get him this far."

I nod my head. "I've done classes with Rex when he was a pup. Though he almost flunked out of behavior training, he did learn a lot." I shift my eyes downward. Rex was a stubborn, obstinate pup and acted out in class. When we all walked with our dogs in a line, Rex danced a little jig and pranced around, holding his head high. When instructed to stop, I'd halt, but Rex would stop a foot in front of me. I'd step forward hurriedly, so it looked like Rex was right at my side. And the command to sit? Rex would look up at me, so I knew he heard me, but he'd take his sweet time in responding. Finally, after many seconds, he'd drop his rear end to the ground.

I wonder if Ryo and Sara will think less of me now that they know Rex and I almost failed in class. *I want to make a good impression. Did I blow it?*

"He earned a D-, didn't he?" Roger adds.

"Right. He was a handful as a puppy and had tons of spunky spirit." I stroke Rex's head. "He's mellowed out over the years."

"He's a great-looking dog," Ryo says, bending down to pet him.

"I'm not afraid to do additional training," I say. "All dogs need it, especially at this young age. Charlie's just over a year, right?"

"Right." Sara watches Charlie walk around the yard. "I hope he shows you his 'Chucky' side while we're here. I want you to see it."

"That would be the aggressive tail chasing mentioned in his bio?" Roger asks. "Charlie Bear, come up here." He pats his legs.

"Yes," Sara continues. "When he's out of his routine and in a stressful environment, he throws fits. It's not a pretty sight. We had people come by to see him, and for two days afterward, he threw fits. But he doesn't seem to be exhibiting that behavior here."

We watch Charlie walk over to Roger, and astonishingly, he jumps into Roger's lap and allows Roger to pet him.

"Well, that's quite unusual," Sara says in surprise. "He usually doesn't want anyone touching him."

Ryo nods her head. "Highly unusual."

I have my eyes on Rex and watch for any signs of jealousy. I bend down, pet him, and whisper in his ear. "You're being such a good boy."

Charlie sits on Roger's lap for quite a while. Roger strokes Charlie gently along the back of his neck, behind his ears, and on the front of his chest.

"What's up with the tail chasing?" I hear Roger say softly to Charlie. "You don't need to do that, you know."

Charlie jumps down to explore some more. This time, Rex chases him around the side of the house and into the garage. I follow and call them both back into the yard. Charlie dashes down the walkway and tears onto the patio. Rex is a ways behind.

All of a sudden, Charlie Bear growls at Rex, and then he snarls. Rex takes it at first, but Charlie doesn't stop. He lunges with pigheaded persistence at Rex's neck. Rex defends himself by snarling and growling in return.

"Hey, stop that!" I yell, stepping in to grab Rex, while Sara grabs Charlie.

"Rex has like sixty-five pounds on you, Charlie," Ryo notes. "You shouldn't mess with him."

"I'm glad Rex growled," Sara adds. "Charlie needs to know his place."

This isn't starting off well at all. We relax a bit once the dogs calm down, but I'm worried.

Charlie Bear leaps onto Roger's lap. I lead Rex a safe distance away.

"We'll have to watch them. It will take time for them to become comfortable with each other."

Little warning bells are going off in my head that remind me of the moments in the old *Lost in Space* television show when the robot moves his arms up and down while intoning, "Warning, warning. Aliens approaching." I shake my head.

"Be sure to feed them in different rooms, so one doesn't go after the other's food," Sara says. "And keep them from trying to play with the same toy, so there's no fighting. Charlie can be possessive."

After a while, Charlie leaves Roger's lap, and both dogs lie down on the patio. Rex is on the rug by the door, and Charlie is about five feet away.

Roger pats his legs again.

"Come up here, Charlie."

He springs right onto Roger's lap without hesitation, like a pogo stick.

"I really like him," Roger declares, looking at me.

I walk over and pet Charlie on the head while he's in Roger's lap. Charlie doesn't seem to mind.

My head is spinning. He sure is cute, and he seems to love Roger.

"Don't forget," Sara adds. "He's on probation for two weeks. Should you decide he's not working out, I will take him back at any time." She walks over and strokes Charlie Bear's head. "Even with all his problems, I still love this little guy."

"Oh, if we decide to take him, we'll keep him," I blurt out. I see Roger look at me.

Ryo adds, "The first two weeks are going to be the hardest—especially with this guy. He's all about routine, and he's not going to like having it messed up. He's going to rebel."

I'm curious how he'll rebel, but I don't ask. This dog needs a home—a forever home. Sure, he has issues. Sure, it will take time for both dogs to become comfortable with each other, but I think a huge dose of love can cure anything. From the looks of Roger with Charlie Bear on his lap, he'll get plenty of that. And I'll make sure Rex gets an equal measure.

"Let's give it a try then," I hear myself say.

"Okay, but don't forget—" Sara adds.

"You'll take him back." I smile.

"I'm not kidding. And don't be afraid to say it isn't working out. He can be more than a handful. He's an obstinate little mule sometimes, and he'll try your patience."

"Oh, I think we'll get along fine," Roger replies.

We walk Sara and Ryo to their car. Roger holds Charlie Bear in his arms; Rex is in the house.

"He likes to go for rides," Sara adds as she gets into the passenger seat. "I enjoyed taking him with me to different places."

We say our good-byes as Ryo starts the engine. They pull away, waving to us as they turn the corner.

"So, Charlie Bear," Roger says, bending his head down near Charlie's ear. "You have a new home here with us."

We walk inside. "We have to watch the two of them together, though," I say. "It would be disastrous if they were to get into a fight."

Roger sits on his recliner, and Charlie Bear jumps up and snuggles on his lap.

I take Rex into the garage, open the cupboard door above the dryer, and pull out a couple of yummy treats for him.

I have doubts about this working out. *Are we making a mistake?*

CHAPTER FIVE

ON THE WEDNESDAY BEFORE we left for our trip, I told my mom we were going away for my birthday. I like to call her at least once a week, and Wednesdays are perfect because the gardeners come that day. Rex always barks at the gardeners; so on Wednesdays, as soon as the gardeners arrive, I grab my cell phone, put a leash on Rex, and take him for a walk in the neighborhood. My mom had asked me to call when we got home from our trip. So at four o'clock on Saturday, after Sara and Ryo leave, I pick up the phone.

"Hi, Mom. It's me."

"Hi, sweetie. You're home?"

"Yup, we're home." I fill her in on the hotel and the show. "We had a marvelous time."

"So what else is new?" Mom asks.

"I got a present for my birthday."

"The trip wasn't your present? What else did your fine husband get you?"

"A dog."

"A dog! What kind of a dog? Don't you still have your big dog?"

"We do, Mom, but remember we lost our cat, Red, a few weeks ago."

"That's right, you told me."

"The house felt empty with only Rex and us; so we adopted a dog today."

"How nice."

"He's a real cutie, but he's a feisty little critter. I'll send you pictures."

After I place the phone on its charger, I step around Rex on my way into the house to see how the guys are doing. Rex is tired. This is a lot of activity for him. He gives me that look where he rolls his eyes without lifting his head.

"Rex, you're a good boy," I whisper.

These days, Rex strolls out of my office in the corner of the house and down the short hallway to the garage, where he has cushy blankets to rest on. I keep the garage side door open for a breeze, which gives him easy and constant access to the yard. During the day, he often has to go out, which has increased in frequency as he's aged. Getting older is the pits.

Inside, I find Charlie Bear asleep in the crook of Roger's arm. We have a busy week ahead, including a gardener day when I'll have two dogs to walk instead of one.

Later, after the guys nap in the recliner and Rex sleeps on his blankets, I call Charlie to go outside. He bursts into the yard with the enthusiasm of a bull coming out of his pen at the rodeo. We watch him sprint around the perimeter and circle a flagpole mounted at one end. He zips by like an Indy racing car. My head spins as I watch him.

I call it Charlie Bear's 500, for he surpasses any racer I've ever seen. He tears circles around the yard, and then he decides his racetrack will include the flagpole, taking the turn one way and then the other. His speed and accuracy are amazing.

"How can he run so fast and for so long?" I ask Roger.

We stand at the door and watch him. He runs his race for a full two minutes.

"It would be great if we could take him to the dog beach," I say. "He'd love it there."

"Rex sure liked it when he was a year old, but we can't take Charlie there until he has more training," Roger adds. "Rex always came when called. He did learn that from his classes. We can't trust Charlie off the leash."

"You're right. Maybe someday though?"

Roger looks at me. "We'd have to trust he'd be good around other dogs first and he'd come to us when called."

"I think that's going to take a while."

"Probably a long while with this guy."

"He's stubborn," I add, "but funny and cute. Look at those ears flop on his head."

"Charlie Bear, come here," Roger calls out.

He prances up to the door like a show dog, and Roger lets him in. His pink tongue lolls in his mouth, making him even cuter as it stands out against his gray, white, and black fur.

After dinner and some quiet time, Rex goes to bed in his room, and we put Charlie into his den in the family room near us. It's a wire crate about three feet by six feet, with a plastic den inside that doubles as a carrier in the car.

While she was here, Sara had told us about the "find it" game. You take little pieces of treats and throw them into the crate at bedtime. He hustles inside to get the yummy treats, and then he lies down to sleep.

"He's tired," Roger says.

Charlie munches on the treats, looks at us, and lies down inside his den, which is lined with a fluffy towel. He rests his head on his white paws and soon closes his eyes.

Roger and I look at each other.

"Piece of cake," I whisper. We don't hear a sound from him all night.

We have the whole day on Sunday to get used to each other. Normally, we don't do much on weekends; we prefer to catch up on watching television or do odd jobs around the house or in the yard. But after our trip this week, we want to relax. Rex is used to our sedate lifestyle. Charlie Bear isn't.

At one point, a bird of some kind chitters in the branches of a tree. Charlie flies out of Roger's lap, races to the door, and runs straight into the screen. Hell-bent and deliberate, he raises his paws, and—*rip, screech, tear*—he tries to scratch, claw, and growl his way through the screen door.

"Charlie! Hold on a second. I'll open the door for you." I jump up and pull open the door, and he dashes into the yard, spunk and grit oozing off of him.

I look at the shredded screen and sigh.

"Strike one, Charlie Bear," Roger calls out to him.

CHAPTER SIX

PERIMETER PATROL. THAT'S WHAT Charlie's foster mom calls it.

"He prances back and forth, on his tiptoes, from one end of the yard to the other," she says in one of her many e-mails. "There's a possibility he has a hypervigilant personality, which is not a bad thing. But I was worried he'd wear himself down."

So this racing around the yard isn't unusual.

"Well," Roger comments as we stand at the door and watch him again, "he gets his exercise."

"That's for sure." I have a sneaky suspicion this kind of behavior is a little obsessive/compulsive, but I don't say anything.

Charlie Bear's issue with being sensitive to touch sure doesn't apply to Roger, and I have no idea why. I wonder if maybe he prefers men? Maybe he had a man who loved him when he was a puppy? Or maybe he senses Roger needs him. Charlie allows me a small pat on the top of his head, but not much more. Roger is able to stroke him and pet him, as long as he doesn't touch Charlie's rear end.

When Ryo found him on the school playground where she works, one of his prevailing issues was the huge amount of dried material stuck to Charlie's rear end. The schoolchildren were circled around, watching a crazy dog twirling around, chasing his tail, and growling and snapping.

"I knew I had to get him out of that situation before he hurt himself or one of the kids," she told me.

She scooped him up, thankful he didn't try to nip at her, and put him in her car. Grateful it was an overcast, cool day, she called a friend to come get him and take him to her house.

When Ryo got home after work, she went to pick him up and cuddle him, but he wouldn't let her. That was when she discovered the hardened mass that pulled and snagged at his fur. "He must have been in incredible pain. He tried to dislodge it or bite it off, but he couldn't reach it. I think that's where the aggressive tail chasing came from."

Ryo knew a shelter would never keep a dog in his condition or with his aggressive, relentless tendencies. That would have been a sure death sentence, so she took Charlie Bear to her vet's office, where they shaved off the mass of tangled hair and dried feces. After the neutering, she took a groggy Charlie Bear over to Sara, her foster, who agreed to take him in. Sara took one look at him and pondered whether she'd have him long at all; he was so darned cute and cuddly.

That lasted one night. When the anesthesia wore off and he awoke the next day, he realized he was in a strange environment with other dogs and people he didn't know.

"That very first morning is when his 'Chucky' side came out," Sara told me. "Chucky is the nickname I gave him over time; it's from the movie *Child's Play*. Remember that loving and sweet doll that turned into a monster in the span of a second? Whenever Charlie Bear didn't get his own way, he'd throw a fit and start spinning, growling, and snapping at himself with increasing intensity. The fits would last a full minute, sometimes more, often occurring several times a day. 'Chucky' is the only way to describe it."

Sara said everything provoked a fit in Charlie—if his food wasn't fixed fast enough, if he was told not to do something, if he was given a command, if he was frustrated, if he was put in the crate, and even if he was touched. She and her husband looked at each other and shook their heads. They didn't know what to do.

"Our two other dogs, Rowdy and Tanner, who are both incredible at reading and speaking dog language, wanted nothing to do with this new dog," Sara said. "Charlie didn't seem to possess the nuances of dog language most dogs grow up with: sniffing protocol, hierarchy of the pack, food and treat regimen. He was clueless and very stubborn."

When I mull over the things Ryo and Sara have said, and what I read in his bio, I should be more concerned about whether this dog is adoptable. *Am I thinking with my heart and not my head?* I can't even watch the commercials on television that depict dogs in shelter cages, whose eyes are pleading for someone to give them a home. They tug at my emotions so badly that I have to get up and leave the room. Rescue and adoption sites make me feel this way as well.

After being left out on the streets and abandoned all those months, this dog deserves a loving environment. He's lucky Ryo rescued him and Sara fostered him. Sara was the stepping-stone to a home for him. Although she said she'd take him back if she had to, it would mean one less dog in the rescue/foster system would be given a chance. She doesn't have the room to take in more than one or two at a time.

Charlie stops his frantic pacing. He begins to growl, and then he snaps and barks at his tail. This goes on for almost a minute, bringing the pitch of his growls and the incessant barking to a crescendo. Nothing instigated it or caused it; nothing bumped into him. It's disturbing to watch. It looks like he's going to hurt himself, though he doesn't actually bite his tail.

"What in the world?" Roger says.

"This must be what Sara referred to when she said he throws fits. After the dried matter was removed, Ryo hoped he wouldn't do it anymore. But he continued to do it, and quite often, at his foster home."

"Charlie, stop it," Roger hollers through the screen.

But he doesn't. We've been cautioned not to use our hands to stop Charlie. His foster dad had done that and been bitten.

Roger steps outside, kneels close to Charlie, and claps his hands together. "Stop it, Charlie."

The loud cracking noise deters him for a moment, and we redirect him to a play toy. But the sessions of "spin cycles," as I begin to call them, continue.

You'd think it would be all strawberries and milk for us dogs after we have been rescued, fostered, and then adopted into new homes. Yeah, you'd think it would be peachy.

Not so. These new "peeps," as I like to call them, are mystified. They think my foster mom is kidding when she tells them I have fits and chase my tail aggressively. They believe that, with enough love, they can help me get over all of my stress-induced habits. They also think that, because I'm so cute, I can't possibly be as unruly as the online site says.

My good looks are the only thing going for me. I mean, hey, look at me! *It's what lands me a gig with these new peeps, and it's what I hear Female Peep say over and over those first few days at her home: "It's a darn good thing he's cute."*

I can only account for my behavior the next night by claiming I'm overtired.

Ever see a toddler scream, throw his or her body on the floor, and kick his or her feet? That's overtired. And that's me.

I walk into my den with ease, and the peeps go upstairs to bed.

Then it happens.

CHAPTER SEVEN

At about ten o'clock, Roger and I climb the stairs to go to bed.

Rex goes to sleep right on schedule. We won't hear a peep out of him unless something menacing, like a raccoon or possum, walks along the wall outside his room.

I call him my great protector. When a solicitor approaches our front door and knocks or rings the bell, Rex lets loose with two or three of his deep barks. I'm elated to have him announce a big dog lives here and not to mess with us.

He's become quite a good sleeper; he even walks himself into his room right at seven thirty, which he does tonight. Using the treat game, we put Charlie in his crate at the same time we did the night before. Everything was the same.

I can't wait to close my eyes and rest. Mornings always come quickly; Roger gets up early to be on the road by six o'clock. I get up too, and make him a couple pieces of toast before he heads out for the day. This past weekend, I didn't get much done around the house, so tomorrow will be for grocery shopping and washing clothes.

As soon as we shut our eyes, it starts. Charlie barks. And it's not merely a single, little bark, but a high-spirited, shrieking, barking session that rivals any coyote family we've ever heard out in the wetlands.

Only a half-mile or so from the edge of our tract of homes is a huge area of undeveloped land. All sorts of wildlife live there. Though I've never seen a coyote on the streets in our neighborhood, we often hear them at night. To me they sound like hyenas with their yipping and laughter-like yelping.

The noises the coyotes make are muted by distance. Charlie's forceful barking is right underneath our room, and it jars our nerves.

"Charlie! Stop it, and go to sleep!" Roger calls out.

He hears Roger, but he doesn't listen. His insistent barks pierce the night.

"Go to sleep, Charlie," I add, thinking he'll listen to a "mother" of sorts.

Ten minutes crawl by. He doesn't stop.

"Can you believe this?" Roger asks.

We lie there in the half-dark of the night. Light filters in through the blinds from streetlamps, and I can see Roger's form in bed. His posture is rigid. With more light, I'd be able to make out his tense jaw and narrowed eyes.

"He'll stop. Give him time," I say. "It's his second night, and he's still unsure of everything." I add a silent prayer.

Another five minutes of barking ensue, and then another five follow that. I keep thinking he'll stop at any moment. Unnerving and unsettling, Charlie's squalls blow away all thoughts of peaceful slumber.

"What in the world did we get ourselves into? Are we crazy?" Roger says.

This is the first indication I've heard from Roger that he might have misgivings about this whole thing. We live a peaceful, serene life. Rex is so well-behaved now. And the cats were never a bother except when Diamond would climb onto the headboard shelf, dislodge the telephone handset from its cradle directly above my head, and send it careening down onto my unsuspecting, sleeping skull. (After several rude awakenings, I put the phone on a nightstand.)

It took Rex a long time to become a mellow dog, but about three years ago, he did. And now we all enjoy each other's quiet company.

I lie in bed and question, *What in the world does Charlie want*? Maybe he has to go to the bathroom, though I took him outside to do that right before his bedtime. I look at the clock. It has been twenty minutes of shrill barking.

"This is crazy, B.J. We can't have this at night."

Roger's voice has an edge to it I don't often hear. When he's angry, he clips his words, and these words now are bitten off and spit out with displeasure.

I throw aside the covers, spring from the bed, and run down the stairs. As soon as Charlie sees me, he stops barking. He sits in his crate, wide-awake. I look at him and in a stern voice say, "Stop it. That's enough."

Three long steps are all it takes for me to reach his den. I open the door of his crate, pick him up, and carry him outside. I snap my fingers, the command I used to teach Rex to relieve himself. With a calm voice, I tell Charlie to go potty. And then I wait.

He sniffs around a bit, looks at me, and then sits on his haunches. He doesn't need to go, but we had to try.

After leading him into the house and putting him back inside his den, I admonish him in a strong voice, "Now, go to sleep."

I turn my back and climb the stairs. Oh, how I pray he'll go to sleep now. If there is anything that will nix this with Roger, and with me too, it's barking at night.

I climb into bed. Charlie is quiet, and I heave a sigh. Then he barks again. I watch the clock. It continues, off and on with diminishing intensity, for three more minutes. Finally, he stops.

"Strike two, Charlie Bear," Roger mumbles.

Chapter Eight

The next couple of nights are better, but not by much. Charlie barks and fusses when put to bed, and our nerves are raw. Then it dawns on me. It's been ten years since Rex was a pup. How could I forget we went through this with him? In fact, it was worse with Rex because he was a very young puppy and not housetrained at all.

I flash back to the many nights of wanting to yell at him to be quiet, to hush already, to stop that incessant, mind-jarring barking that drives us nuts. The training books all say not to rescue or coddle him, to let him bark his way through it, exactly like some parenting books advise parents of babies who cry at night. If there isn't anything physically wrong, let them be, and they'll eventually learn they won't be rewarded for making a fuss.

Of course, I read those books when I trained Rex ten years ago. Ten long years ago when Roger and I were a lot younger and maybe a lot more patient. We've always had our dogs sleep in their own area. They've never slept with us, not even in a crate in our bedroom. We feel if a dog can see us, he'll fuss even more to be let out. I know if we even look at a whimpering or crying dog in his crate, our resolve will break, and we'll let him out. And there would go the training.

Whatever the issues were, we did train Rex, and he grew up to be a wonderful dog, who now goes to bed on his own and sleeps like a charm.

But Charlie Bear is over a year old and way past the puppyhood days of soiling his sleeping area. At this point, it's a matter of who is controlling whom. I suddenly remember what the training books say to do about this problem, and a new evening regimen takes root in our house.

The after-dinner walk. I put a collar and leash on Charlie Bear, and off we go around the neighborhood. I used to do this all the time with Rex. In fact, he went to doggie day care at our friend Nancy's house twice a week, where he romped with similar-sized friends and worked off all that Lab/retriever energy.

On days he didn't go to day care, I'd take him to the dog park. The large, fenced-in enclosure gave dogs the opportunity to run and play, and it was the perfect place to reinforce his training. That was where we strengthened the command to come when I call him. Now, when we go to the dog park, I give Rex a pat on the head when he comes to my side. Then I tell him to "go play" and release him for more fun. We have lots of good times at that dog park and meet many interesting dog owners.

Charlie Bear has too many issues for me to trust him in that environment, even though the park has a small-dog side, separate from the large-dog play area. I'm not comfortable bringing him there yet, so we walk the sidewalks at night for a good twenty minutes. The plan is to tire him out enough to get a good night's sleep.

One early evening, we run into our dog-loving neighbor, Carol. She loves Rex, and pats him lovingly whenever she sees him. She has watched him grow from a bumbling puppy into a well-mannered dog.

"Who is this?" Carol asks. "A new addition to the family?"

She bends down, and Charlie wiggles up to her. "He's a rescue. We got him less than a week ago." I'm amazed at how Charlie takes to Carol, and how he allows her to pet him around his face and neck.

"He's adorable," Carol adds. "Good for you guys. What a sweet family you are."

I pull Charlie away, and we keep walking, getting in those twenty minutes or more of exercise after dinner.

And it works. He barks a little bit the first couple of nights—testing us—but we ignore him, and he quiets down within a few minutes.

Each successive night gets better. Boy, am I relieved. A good night's sleep is a treasure at our age.

That week, on one of our first after-dinner outings, Charlie Bear freaks me out. As we calmly walk along the sidewalk, I dole out high praise to him for staying near my side. Suddenly, a huge, shiny, white truck with monster wheels roars toward us. It's so loud you can hear it before you see it; the tires whine with an ear-splitting shrill. It barrels down the street and is only five feet away from the sidewalk when Charlie, fearless and driven, darts into the street to try to bite it.

"Charlie! No!" I yank him so swiftly I think I make his head spin. I regret it afterward, but if I hadn't reacted like that, he wouldn't have a head.

"Why are you dashing into the street? You could have been hurt."

I reach down and grab him close to my chest. My heart is pounding; his is too.

"What are you thinking? You can't take on a big ol' truck like that. Heck, that thing is one hundred times your size." I inhale and exhale, trying to calm us both. "Man, you could have come right out of your collar."

I walk home with the scrappy little bugger in my arms. "We're going to the store tomorrow to get you a harness."

Charlie's foster mom is right. He loves car rides. On our way to the big pet store, he sits in the passenger seat and doesn't try to come to my side while I drive. I'm impressed.

But when he sees a dog out the window, he bolts upright, puts his paws on the hand rest, looks out the window, and barks loudly. "Charlie, *sh*! It's just another dog on a walk."

We get to the store, and Charlie smells dogs all over the place—in the bushes, by the front door, at the table where the treats are sold, down all the aisles. Rex always has a hard time not lifting his leg, but if I keep his attention on me, he gets through it. No such luck today.

"Charlie, don't," I hiss as I see him lift his leg. Then I see the small, yellow puddle. I look around. My eyes dart to the end of the aisle, and I see a roll of towels with plastic gloves. *Ah, cleanup supplies.* The store employees got smart.

A young employee walks over as I approach the toweling.

"Can I help you?" she asks, noting the puddle. "I'll hold his leash while you clean up."

"His name is Charlie Bear," I tell her, thinking it's quite nice of her to hold him.

I hand over Charlie's leash, grab some toweling and gloves, and bend down.

That's when I hear the young woman say, "Come here, Charlie Bear. Let's say hello to the boxer down this next aisle."

You have got to be kidding. If I could find my voice before they turn the corner and disappear, I'd yell to her to stop. With all the newness happening in his life, I wouldn't put Charlie anywhere near a big boxer. But, not knowing about Charlie's past, this young girl does. And it isn't pretty.

I hear Charlie growl and snap. I spring up from the floor, still wearing a blue plastic glove, and race around the corner. The boxer stands still at her owner's side, calmly eyeing Charlie Bear, who is snapping and lunging at the end of his leash.

"He's a rescue," I say to the store employee. "I'm not too sure about him with other dogs right now." I reach for Charlie's leash. The boxer's owner leads her dog away.

The young girl apologizes and turns him over to me. I hold Charlie on his leash close to my side while I finish the clean-up. We're both agitated; I'm angry with the young woman for not asking me if she could do that, and Charlie is angry at the big boxer. Instead of calming down though, I become furious, thinking there might have been a dog fight. I take a deep breath, push those thoughts out of my mind, and speak softly. "It's okay, you're a good boy. You're sitting here very nicely."

Maybe it's my fault for bringing him in the store, but I need a harness that fits right. We find the aisle where they're located. I pick out a bright red one and try it on him. I want one that's snug but not too tight. I'm amazed he stands still while I put a harness over his head, and then I try a second one, and, finally, a third one. *This is the one*, I say to myself.

I look at the price tag. Boy, at $17.95, it isn't cheap. In this life, most things worth having are worth what you pay for them. Sometimes you pay in time and energy, and sometimes you pay in money. Charlie's safety is right up there as ultra-important, so of course, I decide to fork out the dough.

We stride to the cashier and keep an alert eye for any other dogs.

"What an adorable puppy," the cashier says. "Can he have a treat?"

She holds a small dog cookie in her hand. "Sure," I say, taking it from her. Charlie's hackles are up, and I notice his eyes dart around the store. I don't want him to nip at the cashier or me, so I lay the treat on my open palm.

On the ride home, Charlie puts his paws on the armrest of the passenger side door and leaves little breath imprints on the window. He looks over at me numerous times. "Nope," I tell him, "I'm not rolling down the window. I'm not taking a chance on you jumping out."

When we get in the house, Roger is sitting in his recliner; Rex is by his side. I show Roger the new harness and begin to tell him about what happened when Rex starts to walk toward me.

Charlie lunges at Rex. He snarls, growls, grabs at his throat, and tries to bite him. Just like the first day they met, Charlie comes on like a mad man. A ferocious sound is coming out of this little dog's throat, and he looks vicious. The whites of his eyes show, and his teeth are bared.

Rex is taken by surprise and doesn't have time to react. I drop the shopping bag and the harness and race to Rex's side.

"Charlie, what are you doing?" Furious, I grab him by the scruff of the neck and pull him away.

"What's the matter with him?" Roger asks in alarm.

"I'm not sure, but this has got to stop." I put Charlie into the kitchen and slam the gate across the entrance.

Rex goes into his room, and I follow. "I'm so sorry, Rex. Are you okay?" I kneel down and check him over, but there are no cuts. Charlie's bites didn't land.

"Come over here and lie down on your bed, sweetie. It'll be okay." I put a barrier across the doorway. It's short enough that I can step over it, but it will keep the dogs away from each other. "Rest for a while."

Back in the family room, I fill Roger in on Charlie's behavior at the pet store. "I think he's all riled up from that run-in with the boxer."

I sit for a moment and realize what a difference there is between Rex and Charlie Bear. Outings to the pet store are fun events with Rex. We walk up and down the aisles with ease, not really even noticing the other dogs.

Having Rex socialized so we can walk among people is important. In the course of life with a pet, you're bound to run into people and other dogs, and I like to feel comfortable with my dog's behavior.

It's not always perfect though, and Rex doesn't always behave the way I think he should. For instance, during a ride in the car, Rex will bark at a dog on the sidewalk, but he doesn't bark at that same dog when we pass him on a walk in the neighborhood. That one is a mystery to me, but I've adapted to it. Now, when we're driving, if I see a dog that will soon be in Rex's line of sight, I direct his attention to me, and we pass the dog before Rex realizes he's there. It saves my eardrums from his loud barks in the close confines of the car. I need to do that with Charlie Bear in the car as well, though I wonder if he'll listen to me.

Glancing toward the kitchen, I see an obsessed, hard-nosed, little mutt. He sits behind the gate, quiet and meek.

"His attacks on Rex scare me. I shouldn't have brought him with me, but I had to get a harness that fit."

"Keep them separated," Roger says. "That's all we can do."

That night, tears stream from my eyes as I lie in bed. My first priority is Rex. His well-being comes first. He has been with us more than ten years, and he deserves a life that doesn't include a rescue dog assaulting him for no reason.

With the aggressive snarling, growling, snapping, tail chasing, and attacking, I can't help but consider that this stubborn dog may be unadoptable.

I think about what might have to happen for the good of the household.

Roger called out "strike one" when Charlie shredded the screen door, and "strike two" occurred when he barked in his crate for twenty minutes before going to sleep. I haven't heard a "strike three" from Roger yet, but I can sense it coming. And strike three always means "you're out."

In less than a week, I have developed a stirring of emotion for this little munchkin. I'm not doing cartwheels of devotion, but I do feel sorry for him.

When Rex was a puppy and with us for only eight days, he became terribly sick. We rushed him to a vet, who administered IV fluids and kept him for four long nights, nursing him back to health. He had the parvovirus, a disease many dogs contract in kennel situations. It's often fatal.

I remember crying so hard the sobs wracked my body. I was invested in that little dog's sweet face and gangly legs that bounced around in the yellow flowers in the front yard. Even after a mere eight days, I couldn't picture my life without him.

I went to the store where we got Rex to tell the owner he was sick. After I told her, I was shocked to hear her say, with a toss of her hand toward the kennels, "Pick another one."

I didn't want another one. I wanted this dog, this puppy. Her flippant remark felt insensitive to me, like she considered the dogs to be expendable. That's not how I felt. This puppy was already part of my family. It sickened me to think what might happen to the rest of the puppies in her care.

Charlie Bear's face pops into my mind. He sometimes has a wild look about him, and he shows the whites of his eyes when he's agitated. I've never seen a look like that from Rex. Goldens are known for being compliant and Rex lets me do anything to him: clean between the pads on his feet, wipe inside his ears, and even rub him down after a rain shower. Smaller dogs aren't very compliant until rigidly trained, and sometimes that takes twice as much work.

Whatever I need to do, Rex trusts me and won't react in a strong way. Oh, he'll turn his head away if he doesn't want his ear medication, but he lets me administer it. He even takes a juicy bone from my fingertips by using that "soft mouth" that Labs have; he gingerly closes his teeth around the bone, and then he lets me withdraw it without so much as a whimper or growl.

Charlie scares me. It's quite evident I can't do those same things with him. He has those "issues" of resource guarding, throwing tantrums, and curling his lip when I try to touch him on his paws or his back end. I don't do it much, of course. We're new to getting along with each other, but I worry it might always be this way.

Will he forever isolate himself from me and only allow Roger to touch him? Will he keep ambushing Rex for no reason? Maybe we're trying to give this dog a home when he isn't able to surrender himself to being loved. Is he beyond hope?

I told his foster mom we'd make it work.

But is it too much?

CHAPTER NINE

EGGSHELLS AND BROKEN GLASS—THAT'S what it feels I'm walking on for the rest of the week. When we take Charlie into our home, his foster mom tries to warn us. "Charlie Bear is all about routine," she says, "so we suspect the first week will be tough for him." That's an understatement.

We try our best to set up a new routine for Charlie Bear. In the morning, he's led right outside from his crate and then into the kitchen for breakfast. We put a barrier across the entrance so Charlie can eat on his own and away from Rex. After Roger leaves for work, I take both dogs outside for a little walk around the backyard, and they follow me around the house while I do chores. When I go to work in the afternoon, I separate them. Charlie goes into the gated kitchen, and Rex goes into the garage, each with his own treats. At night, they have their dinners separately again. Then it's cuddle time for Charlie with Roger, while I spend some time with Rex.

On Saturday, I announce what Roger and I both understand. "Today is one week."

Roger strokes Charlie, who is spread out from Roger's lap up to his chin. Charlie finds a place of respite there. He sits calmly and allows himself to be petted.

"So you made it a week," Roger says to him. "What do you think? Can you make it another?"

"Are we going to keep him?" I ask with hesitation. Part of me wants the answer to be "yes," and part of me wants the answer to be "no." I don't want to put Rex in any more danger, yet the Pollyanna side of me has hope, slim and tenuous though it may be, that we can make this work.

"What do you think?" Roger says. "Is he getting better?"

"Maybe a little." I sit on the sofa and tuck my legs underneath me. "He's sleeping better."

"And that's a good thing," Roger answers. "I'm jarring him out of those fits by banging a newspaper on the floor. The loud noise seems to startle him out of it."

"And it redirects his attention. Those spin cycles have come down in number, only four or five each day in the past two days. That's down from almost ten a day in the beginning."

"They're still irritating though," Roger adds.

"His attacks on Rex disturb me the most."

"Me too. We have to keep them separated. During the day, we need to keep them in different rooms."

Roger's look of intensity bores into me. I want these dogs to get along and become friends, but I also know how important it is not to let them get into a fight. Rex's powerful teeth could rip Charlie Bear apart. Even though I don't think Rex would do that, how can we ever know what a dog is capable of when provoked?

I look straight at Roger and answer, "I am. And I watch them with an eagle eye when we go outside. Charlie follows Rex like a shadow."

"Is that a good thing? I'm not sure."

"He doesn't do anything to him; he follows him around. Almost like a player would follow a coach." I remind Roger it was only on that first day that Charlie attacked Rex outside. Otherwise, it has only happened inside the house.

I tilt my head to the side and look at both of them. "Do you want to see how he does in the next seven days? His two-week probation is up on Saturday."

Roger whispers to Charlie Bear, "Can you make it that long without a meltdown?" Charlie darts his little face forward toward Roger's, where he tries to lick him with his tongue.

Roger holds him with two strong hands; he looks at me and says, "Do you want to?"

"I'm all for giving it another week," I say, "despite all his issues."

I look at them together. It's obvious this scrappy little critter adores Roger. In Roger's arms, Charlie turns into that sweet, affectionate, cuddle bear the online bio said he could be.

A girlfriend calls me the next day.

"How's the rescue dog settling in? Does Rex like him?" she asks.

"Rex tolerates him okay, but Charlie is a real stinker."

I fill her in on his rebellious behavior and tell her, "It's a darn good thing he's cute."

I wrap Male Peep around my paw. He falls in love with me on the first day—wish I could say the same about Female Peep. She's all about the big dog. It's only a matter of time before I take over that top-dog spot. I have it all planned. Trouble is, my old issues keep getting in the way.

I guard my food and toys, and I snap at anyone who tries to take them away. I chase my tail whenever I don't get what I want. But these new peeps have a firmness about them. They don't cotton to me ruling the roost, darn it.

And there's something about the touch of that Male Peep that brings out the Charlie Cuddly Bear in me. My foster mom tells them I can be the cutest little snuggler, and it's true. When I want to, I can spread on the charm. And Male Peep laps it up.

On Sunday morning he gets up, has breakfast, and then he goes back upstairs. A few minutes later I hear, "Charlie Bear, come up here."

Music to my ears. I bound up the staircase and run into the bedroom. There's a lump under the covers. I jump up on

the bed, dive onto the lump, and discover it's my Male Peep.
Joy and happiness fill me.

"Come over here, you little monkey," he says.

I weave, bob, and pounce on top of him. It makes him
laugh, which is a sound I like, so I do it some more. After a
while, I hear, "Okay, Charlie. Lie down, and let's go to sleep."

Is he kidding? I'm energized, wired, and wound up tight,
like a tape measure in its case. There won't be any sleeping for
me. Besides, all that excitement has made me want to relieve
myself. So I do. Right here on the comforter on the bed.

Oops.

Chapter Ten

"Come up here, quick," Roger calls out.

I can tell from his tone he isn't in trouble physically, but it sounds like he's shocked at something. I bound up the stairs and enter the bedroom. "What's the matter?" Roger has a towel in his hand and is blotting at a spot on the comforter.

"He peed on the bed."

"What? How'd that happen?" I look at what's left of a yellow puddle in the middle of the white comforter and then grab a towel to help Roger soak it up.

"Maybe he didn't get enough outside time this morning?" Roger asks.

"I think you riled him up, that's what I think. He got too excited." We finish soaking up the mess and then tear the comforter off the bed. "This will have to go to the cleaners. Geesh."

Dry-cleaning a king-size comforter runs about thirty-five bucks.

I look at the two of them. Roger now holds Charlie in his arms, cuddling him close. Charlie's foster mom said she'd hired a dog-trainer to work with Charlie; this trainer told Sara to manage his environment, but we aren't doing that. It's our own fault he climbs up the staircase and onto the bed. We have had him up there before, when we quickly run up for something, but this is the first time Roger has called Charlie and invited him up on the bed.

Out in the garage, I find a board low enough for us to step over and tall enough that Charlie can't jump over it. I prop it across the bottom of the stairs. "Charlie Bear, no more upstairs for you."

I open the screen door. "More outside time," I say to Charlie, and to Roger, I add, "Remember, he's still a puppy. And puppies can't control themselves all the time. You shouldn't call him up there."

Roger looks embarrassed. "I thought he'd snuggle in bed with me."

"Yeah, right." I look at him and can't help but smile. He wants a little cuddle bug, something he can hold, love, and even sleep with. All the dogs in Roger's life have been large, and they never slept in his bed like I used to do with Bogie. The warmth of a sweet pet by your side is comforting. Maybe someday he can sleep with this one snuggled against his chest, but not today.

In the yard, our last remaining cat, Smokey, is crouched on the block wall, waiting to come down for breakfast.

Smokey is the offspring of a beautiful black cat we named Pickles because, on the day she appeared at our door, she was obviously pregnant. After she gave birth in a basket lined with a soft blanket, we nurtured her and her new family, and we asked around the neighborhood to see who this beautiful black cat belonged to.

We found out she was wild and so elusive that she had successfully evaded capture for years.

"We've tried to catch her, so we can take her in to be spayed," a neighbor told me. "But she gets away each time."

I was curious about how long she'd been around. The neighbors weren't sure, but they thought she'd had at least fifteen litters. There are a number of black cats that look like her roaming the area, so I suspected it was true.

Fifteen litters is way too many. Plus, she was adding to the pet population, and there are too many cats languishing in shelters. After finding homes for all except one of the kittens she gave birth to, I made it my mission to help this cat.

It'll be easy to put her in a cat carrier and take her to the vet. At least, that's what I thought at the time.

The first attempt failed miserably. I placed a small bowl of food inside a plastic carrier and set it outside. Pickles stood about thirty feet away with her nose in the air. She glared at the carrier.

"Come on, go in, and eat a little bit," I tried coaxing her to step in. But she wouldn't go near it.

For the second attempt, I ran a string from the carrier's door into the house. I thought, *maybe if she can't see me, she would go inside.* My plan was to close the hinged door by pulling on the string. I used a little tuna on a plate for bait, and she did go all the way in. I pulled the string, the door almost shut, and that was when she went berserk. She threw her enormous size and strength against the door and bolted through it.

Unsure of what to try after that, I called the vet's office. After explaining my dilemma, they told me I could borrow their metal cage with a trap door. It was most often used to catch wild animals that needed medical care. It sounded perfect.

I carried the heavy monstrosity to the backyard. At the vet's suggestion, I placed a piece of chicken in the corner of the cage and propped open the metal door, setting its spring-loaded hinge. All Pickles had to do was approach the bait inside.

What happened next seemed like a miracle.

With a slow, calm, steady gait, Pickles walked straight into the cage, almost as if a loving hand guided her. No backward glance, no hesitation, and no thrashing or trying to escape. Her weight pressed down on the spring, and the door shut behind her.

She sat inside the cage, a calmness surrounding her. She didn't struggle at all.

The vet operated that day, and when I picked her up, she sported a shaved stomach and dissolvable stitches. She was groggy from the anesthesia, so I was advised to leave her in the cage overnight.

The next morning, Pickles awakened and peered at me with big, saucer-like eyes. I let her out at the side of the house; she took a few steps, and then she turned and looked at me. Our eyes locked.

There would be no more batches of kittens every few months, no more foraging for food to feed them, and no more dodging traffic to carry them across the street. I wanted her to have peace. I think she understood that.

We kept the solid-gray kitten from her litter and also had him neutered when he was old enough. Mom and son hung out in the yard from that day forward. They kept an eye peeled for Rex and sprang to the top of the wall when they saw him.

Pickles had a good life after being spayed, and she lived a long time. She lived out her days with her son on one of the lounge chairs in the bright sun. Many years ago, she left us, and now Smokey is the only cat left. He got his name from stretching his gray body up against the glass door on the patio, and we remarked how much he looked like a little bear.

We try to bring him in and make him a house cat, but he meows, scratches at the door, and races back and forth, looking for an escape. He is partly feral and prefers to live outside, so we care for him by giving him breakfast and dinner. When he saunters over to his food bowl, I pet him a little, and eventually, I pick him up and hold him close, feeling the warmth of his stocky, muscular body. Smokey doesn't scratch, but he isn't comfortable being held for very long, and he wiggles out of my arms quickly.

We often see him on the concrete wall, hanging his two legs over the side like syrup dripping down the mouth of a bottle. He stares at the dogs from his high perch. Smokey knows Rex can't reach him up there, and he's learned over the past week Charlie can't either.

Roger joins me at the door. We watch Charlie race to the wall and bound his way up the wall. He stretches up a couple of feet, scrambles down, and stares at the cat.

"Listen up, Charlie Bear," Roger shouts at him. "That cat has been here more than sixteen years. His name is Smokey, and you must respect him."

Charlie turns from the wall, runs to the flagpole, and begins his race. He glances up at Smokey on the turns.

"He's off-limits, Charlie," I add.

Chapter Eleven

The workweek races by, and Saturday, the day I've been calling "decision day," approaches. I correspond with Sara about Charlie's progress—how he's sleeping, his tail-chasing episodes, how he's getting along with Rex—but keep mum about any decision.

"What do you think?" Roger asks after dinner on Friday night. He's referring to the enormous white elephant in the room. But this isn't an elephant; it's a scruffy, obstinate, anxious, salt-and-pepper-colored dog who is turning our world upside down.

I sit cross-legged on the sofa and breathe in, but I don't say anything yet. Charlie is outside; Rex is on his dog bed in what we refer to as his "office."

"I think we should give him back," Roger says.

I look at him, not quite believing what I hear. His voice sounds hesitant and sad. His body language is mixed. He doesn't appear relaxed, and he hasn't turned the television on, which means he deems this an important conversation that needs our undivided attention.

"He's so much work for you. I didn't think about that when we got him," Roger continues. "You walk him each night and keep him apart from Rex, so they don't fight. Behavior training classes will be even more work. I'm not much help after being out on the road all day."

Roger works a long, physically tiring day, getting in and out of his truck making sales calls. My job affords me the luxury of going in to work in the afternoons for a few hours to do the bookkeeping. I'm home with the dogs most of the day, so naturally, I take on the chores. Roger does help out, often feeding them and refilling their water bowls.

I look past him and out the window. Outside, the sun shines bright, and the temperature is a balmy seventy-five degrees. I tug on the sleeves of my shirt and fold the cuffs up, first one, and then the other. I run a hand through my shoulder-length, brownish-blonde hair and tuck one side behind an ear.

Charlie is parked at the door. He's alert and on guard on the mat, which is the greatest vantage point over the entire yard.

I shift my gaze to Roger and say, "That's all true."

"We should have reasoned this through." Roger hesitates, adding, "But it's not too late to change our minds. We have a sedate life with Rex. At almost eleven, he has mellowed out so much."

A myriad of emotions—everything from sadness to fear to anger—begin to churn inside of me. When Charlie is in Roger's arms, content and comfortable, I can see the cuddly Charlie Bear side. But when he snaps, growls, or lunges at Rex with intent and forceful aggression, I am consumed by anxiety and fury.

Will he always be like this? Will he ever get used to Rex and be able to live in our household without attacking him? And if we give Charlie up, will he find a forever home, or will he be labeled unadoptable and be prevented from living a normal dog life?

Back and forth, my mind ping-pongs between a rock and a hard place. This is a big decision.

I exhale through barely parted lips. I try to keep my emotions in check, so I go along with Roger and switch the focus to Rex for a minute. "Remember when Rex was a terror—full of piss and vinegar?"

"He chewed up my reading glasses—was it four different times?"

"And each time he did it, I went to the drugstore and tried to find an exact match so you wouldn't be able to tell he'd chewed them up again."

Roger laughs. "But I always knew. And remember how he'd shred paper by holding it between his paws and gleefully spitting out the pieces? He tore through the house like a banshee, with Kleenex plucked out of the trash!"

"He still does some of those things."

"So what are we doing with a puppy in our lives again?" Roger looks at me with those brilliant blue eyes that sparkle like the sky outside.

"You're right. Puppies are a lot of work." I bite my lower lip and try hard to remain neutral in my heart.

I think for a minute about the pros and cons, and then I answer Roger's concerns. "I'm not afraid of the extra work."

"But it isn't fair to you," he adds.

If this is the only reason Roger doesn't want to keep this dog, we don't have a problem. Sure, this gutsy little guy isn't easy, but neither was Rex. And to think of it in other ways, marriage is a lot of work too. Having kids is a lot of work. Being a loving parent is a lot of work. Even being a grandparent, local or long distance like we are, is a lot of work.

But when I consider the benefits of all those things and all that work, it's really happiness and joy. I don't want to turn Charlie Bear in because he's a lot of work. What bothers me is that I can't trust him.

You see, it's easy to forget about his possessiveness. For instance, when I hold out a small, chewy rawhide bone— one of the bow-shaped ones with the meaty middle—I forget I'm not handing it to soft-mouthed Rex.

"Charlie Bear, look what I have for you." I place the tasty bone down on the floor.

He pounces on it, grabs it between his teeth, and begins to chew.

"Now, let me pick it up, and I'll give it right back. You need to learn I'm in charge of your food." I stick my hand underneath his nose to grab the bone. Instinctively, he bites me.

He snarls a little and even growls before he bites, but I don't get the picture quickly enough. "Ouch, Charlie, what are you doing?"

A pinprick of bright red blood stands out at the tip of my pinky finger. It isn't bad; it certainly could be worse, and I learn a valuable lesson: Don't go sticking your hand under his nose when he has food. I should have known better. It takes time, lots of time, to be able to do that with a dog. Why did I think I could do it in the second week of my time with a rescue dog? Sara told me she had used long kitchen tongs to extricate something from Charlie's paws when she had to.

But including the resource guarding, what bothers me most is Charlie's aggression toward Rex and his incessant tail chasing. These seem like compulsive behaviors I'm not sure he'll ever be able to stop. The tail chasing, snapping, and growling impact only Charlie. It sounds menacing and looks awful to anyone who sees him do it, but he isn't hurting another dog or a person.

The assaults on Rex are another story. They have happened twice. The first took place the day he arrived when he postured for position in the household, and the second occurred after the pet store incident with the boxer. The rest of the two weeks I have kept a constant watch on both dogs, and it hasn't happened again.

But a big *yet* stands out in my mind.

Charlie Bear's issues are not resolved, that's for sure; but I didn't expect them to be in the two-week probation. Sara told me the trainer indicated it would take months, even up to a year, for Charlie to rehabilitate into a dog that is comfortable in a home environment.

I have mulled all of that over in the days leading up to today. I'm not afraid of putting in the time with him, even though Roger thinks it isn't fair. But there's something Roger doesn't see.

This cocky little dog has a complete and utter devotion for Roger. It's something special and something that makes my heart sing. It's the intangible element of love. Charlie makes my husband happy, and that, in turn, makes me happy.

Roger quit smoking on August 11. It was an extremely difficult thing for him to do. I understand the cravings of addiction because I was a smoker into my thirties. I gave it up cold turkey like he is doing now. When he told me he had quit, you could have touched me lightly, and I'd have fallen over. I didn't think he'd ever do it, yet he is still cigarette-free two months and three weeks later.

When you quit smoking, there's still an urge to do something with your hands. And smoking is a stress reliever for a lot of people, so they miss that. It's a strong emotional pull on both fronts. Charlie Bear is Roger's new focus. Now I'm not a doctor, and I don't pretend to have specialized knowledge on what is good and bad for the body; I can only relate what I see. So when my husband sits in his chair with Charlie Bear on his lap, Roger is calmly keeping his hands and mind busy. He talks to Charlie and snips his fur a little around his face so he can see better. When Roger is doing these things, he doesn't have the urge to light up to keep busy.

I want to yell, "Eureka! We've found what will keep Roger smoke-free, and it comes in the form of a little, scruffy, headstrong, rescue dog." Two weeks ago, I considered Charlie a birthday gift for me. But who am I kidding? He's a gift for Roger's health. And with all that love for Roger, it's clear he is Roger's dog.

Roger is still talking while these ruminations race through my mind. I focus now on what he says, but my heart and my head are doing that little wrestling match again. Charlie Bear and I don't have a bond like he has with Roger, but that's okay. Rex is my forever friend—always will be.

As long as I keep Rex safe and give Charlie time to adapt to his new surroundings, I don't mind having him with us. He needs lots of work, patience, understanding, and training to stay consistently on top of his issues. Besides, I can't give up Roger's dog.

"Let's keep him," I say.

"Really? You think so?"

"I do. He'll adjust. We'll adjust. It'll be fine."

Do I know what I'm doing?

Probably not.

Chapter Twelve

We tell Sara and Ryo we want to adopt him. They're thrilled and a little startled, I think, that Charlie Bear makes it through probation. They come to our house with the final papers to sign, pick up the check for the two-hundred-dollar adoption fee and turn over all of Charlie's documentation about his shots, neutering, and microchip. Roger and I think the fee is very reasonable, and we like the idea of giving back to the people who took care of Charlie Bear to help offset a portion of their out-of-pocket expenses.

Sara gives him a sweet kiss. "Be good for these new people, Charlie Bear." She looks straight at me. "Call me if it doesn't work out."

She has those watery eyes again.

"Sara, don't worry."

"I can see he'll get lots of love. Look at him in your husband's lap."

Charlie straddles his back paws over Roger's leg, and his other two paws drape over the arm of the recliner. His face beams with pleasure.

"He's got Roger wrapped up," I add.

Ryo smiles. "When I first saw him whirling and snapping on the school playground, I didn't hold out much hope for his future adoptability. Thank you for taking him in."

"Thank you for rescuing him," I say to Ryo. "And Sara, thank you for putting in so much time and energy in those four-and-a-half months to even get him to the point of potential adoption. You're Charlie's angel."

We don't tell them about our long discussion about whether to keep Charlie. We don't share the misgivings we have about whether he'll ever straighten out with Rex, nor do we confess how frustrated we are with his spinning. We do admit Charlie Bear still needs a lot of work, training, and time—lots of time—to get comfortable here.

Charlie is a work in progress, and he has a long way to go.

We keep the visit upbeat and positive, and we point out the great attributes Charlie Bear does have. We walk Ryo and Sara to the door and say good-bye, and I promise to send updates and photographs.

Our household settles into a grounded routine. Mornings bring playtime for Charlie; we throw a favorite toy, and he runs after it, bouncing from the sofa to the floor and back again. He's a puppy, a willful one, and he needs activity to burn off his energy.

We feed both dogs and give them outside time. After lunch, when I leave for work, Charlie still goes into the gated kitchen. Before I go, I plunk a handful of ice cubes into Rex's water dish in the garage. He loves ice water. Though I try numerous times to get Rex to stay in the house, he prefers his cushy location out there with the breeze blowing. He's content to sleep on his blankets most of the day.

On one of my shopping trips to the pet store, I discover the store sells the Kong toy in mini sizes for small dogs. It's a bouncy, red, nontoxic, natural rubber toy with a hollow center. When stuffed with food or treats, it provides dogs a healthy outlet for a puppy's natural desire to chew and lick. We've always had a large, red, indestructible Kong for Rex. He can chew apart almost anything; he shreds the giveaway Frisbees from pet food stores and the many plastic squeaky toys we give him. But this Kong holds up without a problem. When I leave, I give each dog his own Kong toy with peanut butter in it.

Early on, I discovered the benefit of giving Rex a treasured treat whenever I leave the house. Peanut butter is fabulous. He focuses on the treat—in this case, licking peanut butter on the inside of the Kong—and he doesn't notice that I'm gone for quite some time. It's the perfect way to relieve any stress or separation anxiety. It works for Charlie Bear now too.

Later, when Roger comes home, Charlie jumps onto Roger's lap, snuggling in to be petted. It's the highlight of the day for both of them. And then it's dinnertime.

I institute the "down" command for Charlie before I feed him. He understands basic commands; his favorite one is "down." Even if you tell Charlie to "sit," he'll go straight to a "down."

Interestingly, that's one command Rex doesn't like to do. He'll sit anytime I ask him to. He'll come when I wave an arm toward me and stay when I show him my hand in the stop-sign position. But if I indicate I want a "down" by pointing to the floor or saying "down," he'll merely look at me. I'm mystified as to why he won't do this when he does everything else I ask him to. I wonder if it hurts him. Even as a young dog he could have had joint pain or early arthritis.

The instructor at his behavior training class commented that it was stubbornness. "You'll never get that dog to mind you if he won't do a down." On graduation day, she added a final comment when she handed me Rex's certificate indicating he barely passed, "You're going to have a problem with that one."

Ten years later, I'm pleased to say she was wrong. Sure, Rex doesn't like to do "down." If I coax him long enough with a juicy treat, he might drop to a lying position, but he'll spring right up after he eats the goodie. He often lies down on his own, of course, and rolls over to his side to stretch out. But will he do it on demand? Forget about it. Yet, he's the calmest, mellowest, most obedient dog ever.

Surprised to find Charlie likes to do a "down," I make sure to reinforce it often, particularly when I give him his dinner. We feed the two dogs in separate rooms and pick up their bowls as soon as they're empty. After dinner, I play with Charlie, with his frog toy or stuffed duck. And we go for our after-dinner walk before bedtime.

Comparisons aren't a good thing, and I'd never, ever say one dog is better than another. That would be like saying one of your children is more special or more loved, or one is prettier or more handsome than another. Every child is special.

Of all the dogs I've had the joy of being with, Charlie Bear is unique. Yes, he's young, and he behaves differently, but Charlie Bear sets himself apart in that he is quite the entertainer.

This little imp possesses the personality of what I call the ultimate merrymaker. He grabs a discarded sock, throws it in the air, and races around the room, all while flying from the sofa to the floor to the chair. He does this with the large tops of water bottles too. They make a crunchy sound in his mouth that seems to get him going. He'll also toss a squeaky toy turtle or his little squirrel.

His shenanigans make us laugh out loud.

Charlie has a bottomless supply of energy and lives life with acrobatic zest. But do Roger and I, old codgers that we are, have the stamina to keep up with him?

I try hard to be good every single day. Really, I do. And I'm truly grateful that these peeps took me in, but what's up with Wednesdays around here?

What sounds like a bowling ball being thrown down the lane actually turns out to be a monstrous trash can being rolled down the sidewalk. Then it's dropped at the edge of the curb and lands with a resounding thunk on the street. This happens more than once. Then all the trash cans sit there until a behemoth truck lumbers up, stops, scoops each one up, dumps out the contents, and then smacks them down onto the asphalt. I whirl, run, and frantically pace because the noise hurts my ears and makes me want to run away from it all.

And then there are the gardeners.

"Those are the mow-and-blow guys, Charlie Bear," Female Peep says, trying to console me. "They don't take long."

Those guys pull machinery out of their trucks. First, they untie ropes that bind the machinery in place, and then they pull strings that roar those machines to life. I listen to ear-piercing leaf blowers, screaming mowers, scraping rakes, and spraying water hoses. I don't mind the raking and the spraying, but there ought to be a law against those mowers and blowers.

One day, there isn't any noise at all. The air has an eerily silent calm to it. It's a day in early November, a few weeks after I arrive here. Something doesn't sit right. It's like static electricity through the pads of my feet or something. I'm on high alert, bouncing around and around the yard with my head held skyward. I run up to the screen door and stop short.

That's when it hits.

A 3.8 magnitude earthquake shakes Long Beach, only a short way away.

It knocks the house like someone took a huge fist to it, and then residual waves flow through the ground. They make me a bit unsteady.

Female Peep comes to the door to let me in. "Wow, Charlie Bear, that was a jolter."

I grab my little squirrel and run to the top of the sofa. If you ask me, earthquakes are worse than mowers, blowers, and trash trucks combined.

Chapter Thirteen

The earthquake is one I call a jolter. I can't say I prefer the rolling kind where the earth seems to rush in waves underneath your feet. They're equally disturbing, but at least the jolter is over in a few seconds. The rollers can go on for long minutes and make me feel queasy for a while.

I watch the blinds on the window bang against the wall. It's how I can tell we've had a sizable earthquake. When the blinds finally stop moving, I know it's over. Rex is nonchalant about earthquakes, having lived with them for ten years.

The phone rings later that day.

"Hey, there. How are you?" I recognize my brother's number identified on the phone.

"I'm good. How are you?" Peter's deep voice sounds just like our dad's used to.

"Fine. Are you calling about the earthquake?"

"No, did you have another one?"

"This morning. It wasn't very big though, and we're fine. It was a jolter—one of those that slam into the ground and are over fast."

"I think tornadoes here in Wisconsin are bad enough. I can't imagine living with earthquakes."

"You get used to them. What's up?"

"Mom is in the hospital."

"Is it the fluid around her heart again?" She has been plagued with congestive heart failure over the past few years and has been in and out of the hospital five times in the past eight months. The doctors drain the fluid away each time and send her home, where she rallies for a while before it happens again.

"Yup. She'll be there a day or so. I'm going to see her tonight."

"I wish I could be there," I say. "Is she at the same hospital?"

"Yes. It should be routine, and she'll be out in a day and a half."

"I'll call. Thanks, Peter."

Mom and I chat that night for a few minutes. I tell her again how much I love her and to get well soon.

A few days later, I clutch Charlie's black leash and Rex's red leash in my left hand. Rex's leash is longer, which allows him to move ahead of Charlie in the correct pecking order.

Rex springs forward when we first start out and tugs on his leash, but he slows at about the third street. We culminate our walk with a stop at the end of a dead-end street, where a high fence separates the road from the wetlands on the other side.

When Rex was a tiny pup, he found a hole under that fence and scrambled under it before I knew what he was doing. Dragging his leash behind him, he slid down the embankment into a small stream of water. He thrashed for a moment and then pulled himself up and out. In shock, he came right back up to me, and I dragged him under the fence. The hole was fixed within a week by some other dog owner, who most likely had that same experience.

This is still our favorite spot. Rex is well behaved off-leash now, so I unclip it. I like to let him meander while the breeze over the open land blows into our faces. We often see long-legged white herons perching at the water's edge, brown speckled eagles swooping low over the wispy reeds, ducks and coots bobbing in the murky water and a few trucks carrying workers to the oil rigs that dot the landscape. Black gold is what they called it years ago, and drilling rigs still dot the landscape here and there. There are even some in the backyards of a few houses in our subdivision, while at least half a dozen off-shore rigs light up our stretch of Southern California coastline at night.

Farther down in this area, about a half mile away, is an access point where I used to take Rex for long walks on the sandy hill. Rex loved to race ahead of me, romp and weave his way up and down, and then tear back to my side. But that was years ago, before Rex suffered a torn ACL.

I let him wander, while I hold Charlie's leash and talk to Mom on my cell phone.

"Hi, Mom, how are you?"

"I'm home from the hospital."

"Are you resting? Those hospital visits take a lot out of you."

"I'm fine, sweetie," Mom adds, "getting my strength back."

"You should take it easy."

"I am," Mom says in a small voice. "So what's new?"

"Well, this new dog—"

"That's right; you have the new rescue dog. What's his name again?"

"His name is Charlie Bear, and he's very different from Rex."

"Well, of course he is," Mom says. "You've had Rex a long time."

"Ten years. He's so well-behaved, and he minds me." I think about Rex's life as an incorrigible puppy. He chewed. He dug. He barked. He had unruly behavior; and yes, it took a long time for him to mellow out and become less impulsive. It came around the age of six or maybe seven. Will it take Charlie Bear that long?

"No two dogs are the same." Mom chuckles a little on the other end. "Remember all the different ones your father brought home from the gas station? The ones people abandoned in the restrooms?"

"Dad found homes for them with his customers. All except for Bogie, whom I begged Dad to let me keep."

"Bogie was cute. You said Charlie Bear is little too, right?"

"He's only seventeen pounds. Rex is eighty."

"You can't compare apples to oranges," Mom says. "When are you coming up here again?"

"I can't say for sure, Mom." I lead Charlie from the top of the mounded hill to the bottom. "Maybe in the spring."

"That's so far away."

I try to get up there twice a year, which is as much as I can manage with the cost of airfare, a rental car, and the fact that I have to work. In August, I flew up to visit, stayed almost a week, and took Mom to a lovely hotel for a few nights, where we enjoyed a family reunion of sorts with some of my siblings and their kids.

"Well, you must have to go. Call me again, okay?"

"You bet, Mom. I love you."

The gentle wind swirls my hair into my face as I envision Mom's sweet smile. The memory of her soft kisses on my cheek when we say good-bye pulls at my heart.

I tuck the cell phone into my pocket. "Come on, Rex. Let's go." I clip on his leash.

CHAPTER FOURTEEN

ON A SATURDAY MORNING the second week in November, I have a group of women over to the house for a meeting in which we work on writing stories for submission to magazines. We get together every three weeks and have been doing so for almost fifteen years.

We rotate the meeting's location among the eight of us, and it's my turn to host today. They arrive one or two at a time and are eager to see this new little munchkin we've added to the family. Charlie Bear loves the attention as they bend over to pet him. He jumps as high as he can, but he barely reaches a person's knees.

"Don't pet him if he jumps up," I say. "Ignore him until he quiets down. And don't touch him near his rear end. He's sensitive there."

As long as Charlie is soliciting attention, he laps it up. My friends laugh at his overt attempts to be petted. When they sit in their chairs, Charlie puts his paws up on their legs, wags his tail, and pleads with his eyes. It's amazing how Charlie Bear loves the petting from the women in the room and from Carol, across the street. But he doesn't jump up for loving from me. Is he jealous of the attention I give Rex?

Rex brings his pink blanket into the room and shows off his calm, quiet demeanor. They've all met Rex, and after hellos and head rubs, Rex walks into his room on the other side of the house.

The doorbell rings. It's the last two women to join the group. I fling the door open wide, welcome them, and give them a warm hug. I barely register Charlie around my feet, but when I do, I see him look out the open door at the green grass, the sidewalk, the street, and the wide-open space of freedom.

Before I know it, he wiggles past the last woman, steps over the threshold, and glances up at me. Then he looks down the driveway and up at me again.

"Come, Charlie Bear. Inside."

He doesn't listen. What puppy would listen without being trained? It's stupid of me to think he'll mind like Rex would if I'd told him to come.

Charlie takes off.

He races down the driveway and makes a quick left. His feet shred the concrete. If I clocked him, he'd register twenty miles per hour.

He looks at me once, but then he keeps going. "Charlie, come here," I yell.

I race after him. He sees what's coming. A wall. He doesn't realize he's in a cul-de-sac. I figure *I have him. This is it; he isn't going anywhere*. But he's undaunted. He makes a U-turn, crosses the street, and flies up the sidewalk on that side.

"Come here, Charlie. Come here." My heart thumping in my chest, I run after him. It rained this morning, and the streets are wet. The little footie socks on my feet, which Charlie loves to play with when I'm not wearing them, are soaking wet. He races down the sidewalk, tail held high. His little body is flying.

Now he's at the opening to our dead-end street, where there is lots of traffic.

What have I done by letting him get out? He could get hurt. He could be killed.

"Charlie Bear, NO!" The rascal is fixated on one thing only, and that's running. He darts right into the street, not slowing a bit. I turn my head left and then right, praying there are no cars speeding toward us.

Then I see a welcome sight. Carol stands outside her front door directly across that busy street.

I shout to her, "Call him to you, please!"

Carol puts her arms out wide, kneels down, and says, "Come here, Charlie. Come here."

The nervy little bugger won't turn down loving from Carol. He runs right up to her, and she grabs him.

"Thank you so much," I pant.

"How's Rex getting along with the new baby?" Carol asks.

"Okay."

"He sure is cute."

"And a handful."

"They always are as puppies. Aren't they?"

"Thank you so much for calling him to you. You're a lifesaver."

Carol ruffles the top of Charlie's head. His tongue's hanging out, and his body is panting. "You stay near your home, little guy."

"Thanks, Carol."

I hug the troublemaker tight to my chest; I can feel both our hearts hammering. When I set him down inside the foyer, he scrambles off to the kitchen for a drink of water.

A memory flashes in my mind of a golden Lab sprinting down that same street when he was a puppy. A younger me was chasing him. He raced to the end of that same cul-de-sac with his tail held high, his ears flopping, and his body flying like the wind.

It seems I've forgotten a lot of things puppies do.

My guests are chatting, pouring coffee, and getting glasses of ice water. They never even discover I've had a little adventure. I peel off the wet footie socks, put on a new pair, and join the group at the dining room table.

While I listen to the flowing conversation, I make a promise to myself not to let that ever happen again. It scared me to pieces.

Chapter Fifteen

By the second week in December, the holiday season is upon me with a rush. My life revolves around buying, wrapping, and shipping gifts to out-of-town family. With a large number to send, everything has to be accomplished by this time or the post office claims the gifts won't arrive on time. That's okay because I like to get presents out early, especially to the grandchildren. When I was a kid, I remember noticing the presents under the Christmas tree that had different wrapping paper. That meant those presents were from out-of-town relatives.

My siblings and I used to shake the rogue boxes, almost always finding a rectangular one that held clothes of some kind. The pleas began as soon as the gifts arrived.

"Mom, Dad, can we open them now?"

"No, you have to wait," they always replied.

"Please? Can we open just one?" My two sisters and I—and later, my brother as well—joined in a never-ending chorus. Like Alvin and the Chipmunks, one of the great singing groups of our day, we wore Mom and Dad down.

"Come on, please?" we asked again and again.

Their resolve broke. "You can open the out-of-town gifts on Christmas Eve before we go to church."

"Yippee, hooray," we sang out and jumped for joy.

After late afternoon mass, Christmas Eve always meant an elaborate spread of goodies, from simmering sloppy joes to fresh vegetables and dip. There were potato chips with onion dip, always a big plate of brownies, and green and black olives. The kids weren't supposed to eat the black ones because they had this cool, perfectly rounded hole on each end. They were the exact size for the tops of each of our young fingers.

We wiggled them around at each other and made a heck of a spectacle, chasing each other in the kitchen. Mom considered it playing with our food—which, of course, it was—and Dad didn't like it because he loved black olives. After fooling around, we bit off the tops of each olive. Starting with the pinky finger, we worked our way over to the thumb. After that, we devoured the remaining pieces stuck on each finger. But the tippy-tops tasted the best.

"Hey!" Dad shouted a short while later, brandishing the empty olive bowl above his head, a sly smile across his face. "Who ate all the black olives?"

Platters of food covered the countertops, buffet style. Some brought a dish to share; others didn't if they couldn't afford it. The house was filled with family, friends, Dad's employees, and anyone who didn't have a place to go. Dad's customers at the gas station were always invited and welcome in our home.

Along with all the relatives and friends, there were at least two or three family dogs. They jumped around with the little kids, staked out their place under the kitchen table or near the sofa in the living room, and hoped for a fallen cookie.

It was even more fun when Dad hired a Santa Claus.

"Ho, ho, ho, Merry Christmas," Santa yelled from the doorway to the living room, a red velvet sack slung over his shoulder.

After gathering all the children around him and with the adults watching from the sidelines, he unpacked his sack and called out names, never missing a single person (or dog) in the room. I marveled at how there was always a present for everyone, and Santa always knew to ask a very important question.

"Does anyone have a birthday today?" asked Santa.

"Yes," the children shouted.

Grandma B., Dad's mom, wearing her furry red robe and fluffy white slippers, sat on Santa's lap while we all sang a resounding chorus of "Happy Birthday to You." It was fitting that this sweet, compassionate woman had a birthday that ushered in the birth of Jesus the next day.

It wasn't until I was a married woman and the mother of two children that I learned Santa's secret. Dad put the gifts outside our back door for Santa to put into his sack. On the gifts, Dad wrote the name of each child, adult, and pet in the house. He purchased extra things, like toiletries or beauty aids anyone could use, and he labeled them right before Santa arrived. He also reminded Santa to ask about Grandma B.'s birthday.

It was a merry, merry time filled with joy and laughter.

Those memories flood through me while I put the final touches on gifts to mail. Mom is at the top of my list. She misses the celebrations of long ago more than I do. She's alone now; Dad passed away years before, and all her children are spread out around the country. I get ready to wrap a cute, plush owl and a book of Christmas stories I think she'll like.

Earlier in the season, my brother called to say Mom is in a senior-living facility after another congestive heart failure episode. The doctor, concerned by Mom's inability to bounce back after her last hospital stay, recommended a place where she'd receive around-the-clock care.

Now, I pull the cordless telephone from its cradle, plug in a hands-free headset, and dial the nursing home where Mom lives. Charlie Bear looks up at me from his stretched-out position on the living room rug. I ball up a discarded piece of wrapping paper and toss it to him. He tackles it with fervor.

The dining room table is my wrapping station. It holds tissue, rolls of paper, ribbon, and bows. I spread out a roll of festive paper and listen as the phone rings. A nurse answers and puts me through to Mom's room.

It's hard being so far away from family, especially at holiday time. Mom lives in Wisconsin, which is where my brother, my oldest son, and my two grandsons live. I cut the paper to wrap one of Mom's gifts. A hear a small voice say, "Hello?"

"Mom, how are you?"

"I'm okay, sweetie," she responds.

The ribbons, vibrant red and emerald green, shine bright in the sunlight streaming in through the window. Mom sounds weak and frail; I can hear it in her voice.

"Are they taking good care of you?" I close my eyes and say a prayer. The staff will do their best, but I want to hear her answer. She doesn't like all the fussing—the constant poking and jabbing—and I can only hope she'll focus on the good things about being in a facility where she'll receive constant care.

"Yes, they're very nice. And they're taking good care of me."

Her voice sounds so far away.

I drop the ribbon and book, plop onto the sofa, and curl my legs under me. An image of Mom's small frame in a huge hospital bed overwhelms me. My brother says she's lost so much weight that her hands and arms are bird-like. And I know she's covered in more bruises, like the ones she had in August when I saw her. She bruises not only from the needles where her shots are administered, but also from normal bumping into things around her tiny apartment. Deep purple splotches mar her arms from her wrists to her elbows and above.

"Mom, I miss you."

"I miss you too, sweetie, and I love you."

She always says that. Always.

"I miss you too, Mom. And I love you very much." I don't want to keep her on the phone long, but I also don't want to hang up. "I'll call again, Mom. Get better, okay?"

"I will. Love you," Mom says again.

"Love you too. Bye." I press the "off" button and tear the headset from my ear. I wrap my arms around my legs, pull them up to my chest, and try to send all the love I can to Mom, who is two thousand miles away.

There's nothing I can do but pray. God has her wrapped in His loving arms. That should comfort me, and it does, but I still think, *if only I could be there.*

Later, I call the nurse's station, thank them for taking care of Mom, and walk to the dining room table. There sits the gaily wrapped book. I pull out white tissue paper infused with colored glitter and roll the little owl inside of it. A spool of bright yellow ribbon beckons. I snip off a long section, tie the ribbon around the wrapped owl, and use scissors to curl each long strand.

I place the owl and the book inside a small brown box and then address it to Mom at the nursing home. At the last second, I slip a holiday greeting card inside to add a festive touch to her room. I already sent one to Mom's apartment, but I'm not sure she's seen it because it takes almost a week for mail to make it across the country.

Chapter Sixteen

A MONTH AFTER ROGER quit smoking, I told him that if he stayed smoke-free, I'd buy him a cake each month for a whole year.

I have "Congratulations! Four months!" written in icing on top of the cake. Then I sneak it into work that afternoon. With four lit candles stuck into the frosting, I call the other two employees to join me, and I carry the cake into Roger's office.

"Congratulations!" I say. "Make a wish."

The cake isn't a surprise. But Roger's grin, partly from embarrassment at having attention drawn to him, brings me happiness and joy. Maintaining his commitment not to smoke is a huge accomplishment.

Charlie Bear's two-month anniversary of being with us rolls around five days later. He still runs his Charlie Bear's 500 in the yard, still spins, and he still guards his food and toys. There are no more episodes of assaults against Rex, and the two dogs are coexisting peacefully. For now.

I have my fingers crossed this good behavior will continue.

Nothing much changes here in December as far as weather is concerned. For the most part, the days are sunny and mild. The nights get colder, and the mornings are frosty—if you call forty to fifty degrees frosty. I find an extra sweater and some slippers to see me through the chill in the house. It's certainly nothing compared to the boots, mittens, scarves, hats, and winter coats needed to brave the outdoor weather in Wisconsin. I don't miss chipping the frozen ice on the windshield of my car before leaving for work, or sliding on a slippery road trying to make it to the grocery store. I struggled for many years in that freezing weather, having moved to California in my forties after meeting Roger.

I do miss the beauty of the snow when it outlines the bare branches of trees and stacks up high on mailboxes. There's something about the pristine look of a newly snow-covered landscape that makes the world look promising and peaceful.

You can tell Christmas has arrived in Southern California when colored lights adorn the exteriors of many homes and parking becomes a competitive sport at the mall. The average temperature at this time of year runs from a high of seventy degrees to a low of around forty. And while it's never cold enough to snow, we do our best to have a festive atmosphere for Christmas. We hang strings of white lights across the façade of our home and around a small tree on the front lawn. Roger tacks up large, red, velvet-covered bows over the doorway, on the mailbox, and on each pillar at the side of the garage. The house is festive. A large, green holly wreath on the door is the perfect final touch.

I enjoy the blinking displays of icicle lights on many houses in the neighborhood and the nativity scenes displayed on some lawns Charlie and I see on our walks. But there's an animated display of lights that whips Charlie Bear into a frenzy. It's a set of deer that features one standing and the other lying prone on the grass. Both swivel their heads to and fro; the small, white lights twinkle and move with them.

Charlie barks and tries to lunge at the deer, which makes me laugh.

"Charlie, they're fake."

That doesn't calm him. We hurry past the home. He looks back twice and emits a guttural growl.

A trip to the pet store is a holiday tradition, and this one promises to be extra fun. I have two furry "kids" to buy for, one like an older brother to the other.

Stockings filled with festive pet toys summon shoppers. Bright ribbons adorn the stockings. I find a bag of Charlee Bear treats and think that's pretty funny, so I buy them for

Charlie's stocking. For Rex, I pick out a pack of rawhide chewies he loves.

I wheel my cart up and down the aisles. By the time I'm through, my basket is filled with practical presents, such as dog food and new water bowls, as well as extravagant packages of stuffed squeaky toys and treats. The total cost, $57.86, springs up on the cash register. I can't believe I spend that much, yet I do have two bags of dog food along with all the gifts.

One year, I wrapped Rex's present and placed it under the tree. Roger came down the stairs and asked, "What's he got?"

I was in the kitchen, taking a tray of cookies out of the oven. "What?"

"He has a wrapped present, and he's opening it," Roger declares.

Rex held the package down with his paw while he methodically tore the festive paper with his teeth. He had spit the pieces off to the side.

"Geez, Rex, not again." I walked over and grabbed what was left of the wrapping paper, the ribbon, and the gift. He hadn't torn into the plastic bag of treats yet.

"Rex, you have to wait for Christmas."

He stares up at me with a quizzical look.

"Not yet, Rex."

I placed the bag of treats on top of the refrigerator and rewrapped them later.

This year we have two dogs. I sneak the bag of surprises from my shopping trip into the house and surreptitiously show Roger what we bought them.

"Don't wrap them and put them under the tree," Roger says. "Charlie has a nose like a bloodhound."

"Rex does too." I grin.

Chapter Seventeen

The telephone rings at twelve thirty on the morning of December 20. When I get the phone to my ear and the woman on the other end confirms who I am, she says, "Your mother is not breathing." I blink my eyes rapidly and try to clear the sleepiness from my head.

"What do you mean she's not breathing?" I manage to say.

"We're doing the breathing for her right now, but we need to know what you want us to do."

The nurse had tried to call my brother, who is listed as the person to call for medical directives, and she even talked to my aunt, my mom's only sibling. But my aunt said she wanted to talk to one of us, my mom's kids, first.

When I was there in August, I had a discussion with Mom about her desire for care, and she told me she didn't want heroic measures keeping her alive.

"Feeding tubes? Ventilator?" I asked.

"No. None of those. If it's my time, let me go."

Peter and I talked about this a few days ago. Mom had told him that each time the fluid made it so she couldn't breathe, she became more and more afraid. And she found it difficult to regain her strength after each episode.

"She told me she's tired," Peter said. "Tired of fighting."

I sit straight up; my hand clutches the phone. I picture Mom, frail and small, surrounded by doctors and nurses trying to keep her alive. "You can't reach my brother?"

I don't know if they have a Do Not Resuscitate order on record, and I don't think to ask.

"No, we've tried. He's not answering his phone."

"Can I call you back?" I have to speak to my brother or my aunt before I can tell this nurse anything.

"Yes, but do it soon. We can't wait much longer."

Roger and I look at each other. I fill him in quickly and then call my aunt. She confirms what I already know. No heroic measures. She offers to call the nurse to tell them to let Mom go. Relieved, I agree because it would be very hard for me to do that. I hang up the phone, close my eyes, and pray.

My aunt calls a few minutes later. "She's gone. I'm so sorry."

My aunt tells me Mom had been brought to the hospital earlier that evening from the care facility because the doctor suspected pneumonia. With all of Mom's medical problems, this wasn't unexpected. And we all knew that.

In shock, we mutter platitudes of "She's at peace now" and "She's in a better place," words that should bring comfort, but at that moment, they can't undo the sadness I feel. I hang up the phone, and Roger holds me.

Are we ever truly ready to let a loved one go? Are we ever prepared for the shock of not seeing her again, holding her close and kissing her on the cheek?

My dad died from complications of emphysema in 1997. He was sixty-nine. That was young, too young, but there are others who die much sooner. I was blessed to have him in my life as long as I did. His death drove home the stark reality that our bodies don't hold up forever.

Sickness, disease, and old age claim many, and sometimes, without any warning, a person is gone in an instant.

I often have what I call "the great debate" in my own mind. Is it better to lose someone in an instant or have the person linger, giving you time to say good-bye?

When I was a teen, my older sister and I dated two best friends. The four of us went swimming in a lake where my folks had rented a cottage for a week.

"Last one to the raft is a rotten egg," my boyfriend, who later became my first husband, shouted.

My sister was the first to get to the raft anchored a ways from the shore. I climbed up right after, and my boyfriend soon joined us. My sister's boyfriend never made it.

"Oh, he's such a prankster; he's probably hiding behind the raft," my sister said.

We scanned the water and the shoreline but didn't see any sign of him. By the time divers found him at the bottom of the lake, it was too late. He had been the victim of a strong undercurrent.

He was only twenty-one. One minute he was here; the next he was gone.

Dad suffered a stroke after routine surgery and became paralyzed on one side, but he lived for seven more days. I was able to talk to him, read to him, and tell him again how much I loved him.

The great debate rages in my mind because if I had my choice, I'd choose neither. I want all those I love to be here always. But that's not the way things work. Raised in an Italian household, I attended Catholic school and went to church every Sunday. I believe God is waiting in heaven to welcome his children home, and we are all called there when it's our time. After the drowning, I learned to value every moment with loved ones and to treasure parting good-byes, like those I had with my mother when I left her side and flew home to California.

They say life is a gift and there is nothing like the present.

Tonight, I have deep sadness, but no regrets. Mom knew how much I love her. I told her often, and she told me. I spent quality time with her, and we made memories that will last the rest of my life. I have photographs of her laughing and raising her glass at her eightieth birthday party. There are pictures of Mom wearing her aqua bathrobe and matching flip-flops when she joined us at the hotel pool for a dip in the Jacuzzi. And I'll never forget the joy on her face when we sat in the booth at Culbert's Custard and we shared a double-scoop ice cream sundae with hot fudge, whipped cream, nuts, and two cherries on top.

The sadness isn't because she's called to heaven; it's because I'll no longer see her smile or watch her laugh and giggle like a schoolgirl.

Roger's strong arms wrap around me, and I raise my head from his shoulder. "I need to call my sisters," I say. I creep down the stairs. Charlie is asleep in his den; Rex is in his room. I pull the phone off its charger in the kitchen and carry it into the living room, where I huddle on the sofa and pull my legs up to my chest.

I punch in the number of my sister in Georgia. It goes to voice mail. I try my brother again—voice mail there too. I leave messages, sigh, and look at the clock. In a few hours, they'll be up, including my other sister, who lives in Florida.

I let my body sink into the soft cushions of the couch, pull the throw blanket over my legs, and close my eyes. Sleep doesn't come. I think of Mom's wide-open arms as they welcome me when I visit, the little smiley faces she draws on each card she sends, and the silly jokes she likes to tell and retell. Tears sneak out and land on the maroon pillow.

The next morning brings a flurry of phone calls about funeral arrangements, airline reservations, and all the other matters involved when a parent passes away. Mom specified all of her wishes, even down to paying for her service and her burial plot at the cemetery.

With Christmas five days away, we all have plans in place for the holiday. A conference call brings out raw emotions and gut reactions.

"I'm getting on a plane," one sister announces.

"But we haven't made any arrangements yet for the service or anything," I say in a soft voice.

"So, I need to get up there," she responds.

"But she's not there," I say. "There's nothing we can do for her."

I close my eyes and listen to the soft cries, my heart breaking.

After a while, I speak again and try to be the voice of reason, reminding them Mom would want us to celebrate the holiday with our children and grandchildren. "She wouldn't want to be the reason Christmas isn't celebrated this year," I say and pause. "And I don't think it's fair to friends of hers to schedule her service on Christmas Eve, or even the day after Christmas. Do you?"

"So when then?" my sister asks.

"Peter, can you go to the funeral home and ask them if we can set it for the twenty-ninth or the thirtieth? I'm thinking of flying up there the day after Christmas."

We all get through the holiday weekend. Though for me, it's hard not to call Mom, like I always have, to wish her a Merry Christmas. She used to spend the day with her sister and all the kids on that side of the family, so she was never alone. Still, I miss her voice and the way she always said, "I love you, sweetie."

Roger isn't coming with me to Wisconsin. He'll stay behind for a couple of reasons. First, Charlie Bear has only been with us two months. To leave him in someone else's care for almost a week would send him into a tailspin, and we already have enough of that. He's all about routine. We could ask Sara to take him into her foster home, but we don't want to confuse him. He's getting used to us and his new home.

Roger makes it clear he'll come with me if I need him, and I thank him for thinking of me. But the second reason he stays behind is because my siblings and I have so much to do, and we only have four days to do it. We have to plunge into taking care of all of Mom's things in her apartment. There's a sofa, end tables, a television, her queen-size bed, a small air conditioner, an oak dining table and four chairs, and clothes and cupboards and closets to go through. It wouldn't be fair to leave it all to our only brother to handle.

"Thank you for wanting to be there for me." I look at Roger and at Charlie in his lap. "But I'll be fine. I have lots of family there, and I'll talk to you every day."

"You're sure?"

"I'm sure. You take care of Charlie Bear and Rex. Knowing they're both getting the care they need is important to me. And I can work hard with my brother and sisters to get things done."

The day after Christmas I board a plane and land that afternoon in Wisconsin. When all of us are reunited at Mom's apartment, we hug, cry, and wipe away tears.

"You know," a good friend said to me earlier in the week, "isn't it just like your mom to have a reason for her four kids to see each other during the Christmas season?"

It's bittersweet.

All of our spouses stay behind, which gives us time to grieve and be together. Over the next few days, we sort through knickknacks, cupboards, and drawers.

"Does anyone want this tea set?" someone asks.

"You can have it," says another.

Once we reach Mom's bedroom, we find her extensive collection of jewelry. It's mostly cosmetic, but some of the pieces hold a special place in our hearts.

"She wore this all the time," says one sister. "I'd like to have it."

"I want that too," says another.

"Flip for it," Peter says. "Put the jewelry you all want out on the table and draw a number. The person who draws number one picks an item first; the person who draws number two goes next. You get the idea. It goes around like that until all of the jewelry is gone."

"You have to be included too," my younger sister states.

"Fine, include me," Peter says. "I can save the pieces for my daughters."

Over the next few days, I embrace oodles of mementos—a favorite necklace, a bracelet, a figurine Mom kept on a shelf in her kitchen—and they give me comfort. All are reminders of her loving and giving spirit. Tears and emotions boil over at the smallest remembrance as we hold special items close.

Whatever we don't want or can't use we set aside for donation.

Four days later we lay Mom to rest, and the day after, on New Year's Eve, I arrive home in California. The year comes to a close, and instead of celebrating the New Year with a bang, I usher it in with a whimper. The losses of Diamond in February, Red in October, and Mom in December hit me like punches in the stomach. I'm determined 2011 will be a much better year.

CHAPTER EIGHTEEN

I PLUNGE INTO WORK with a vengeance, answering e-mails, returning phone calls, and responding to the many friends who send condolences and cards.

I go through the motions, taking care of the house and fixing the meals. And it's not until later that I realize how much Mom's loss affects me. I no longer have a living mother or living father. Sure, many of my friends have already lost their parents, but until it happened to me, it seemed distant, far away, and unlikely to happen.

Maybe I even speculated it would never happen, but of course, it would. Mom had been getting sicker, and though I knew the end was near, my heart wasn't ready to believe it.

One day, I find a package stuffed into my mailbox. Tugging it out with the rest of the mail, I bring it into the garage, slit the tape on the sides, and pull open the top. Inside, wrapped in sparkly white tissue paper, is a stuffed owl, the orange eyes bright and cheery. Next to the owl, wrapped in shiny paper adorned with reindeer, snowmen, and cheery red Santa Clauses, is a book of Christmas stories.

I lean against the washing machine and look closely at the box. It's marked "return to sender." Mom never received the gifts. She never got to open them.

I put my hands over my face and try hard to hold it in. My stomach contracts, tears squeeze out, and convulsions start. I can't hold it inside anymore; it bursts forth in sobs and rivers. My nose drips; my eyes burn; my stomach hurts; my head aches. I let myself go. I let the grief take my body in waves.

Eventually, my sobs subside; the convulsions stop; the tears become trickles. I kneel down and put my arms around Rex. He buries his face into the side of my neck. I remember how Mom wrapped me in her arms, and Rex's warmth comforts me.

I cradle the little owl to my chest. I will always miss Mom, but she's forever in my heart.

In early December, I had bought a calendar for the new year. I chose one with squares big enough to write in. Flipping through all the months, I made notations for birthdays, anniversaries, and special occasions, and I hung it inside the cupboard door in the kitchen so we could see it each morning.

Even though the calendar is right there, I almost miss Rex's big day, a red notation with a heart around it on January 10. It's Rex's birthday, and he turns eleven. We give him extra bacon treats and a big rawhide from his Christmas stocking, and we sing "Happy Birthday to You."

In the pet adoption community, they say a dog placed into a new home often gets "three month-itis," moving from good behavior at his new place to testing the waters once again. Charlie's behavior hasn't been that good to begin with. Sometimes I catch Charlie slunk back on his haunches looking at Rex with an obvious intent to lunge forward. It's frightening. I separate them immediately by calling Rex into his office and Charlie into the kitchen.

Charlie's three-month mark occurs right after Rex's birthday. If Rex avoids Charlie or gives him wide berth when they go through the door or falls behind and lets Charlie go first, it's an indication something isn't right. I try to be hypervigilant about their time and space together, but this happens right around the time I open that undelivered box of Christmas gifts. Maybe I'm not paying enough attention. Maybe I've let things slide a bit. Maybe I'm preoccupied, and my head isn't clear. Whatever the reason, Charlie has a meltdown.

Charlie attacked Rowdy and Tanner, the dogs at his foster home, and though he didn't hurt them, the dogs began to give Charlie wide berth when they were around him. Charlie also attacked Rex two times. Once in a while, he'll growl at Rex, but he doesn't rush him or try to bite him. But one night after dinner, when Roger is in his recliner and Charlie Bear is on his lap, I walk through the family room with Rex. Charlie looks at Rex, growls, springs off the chair, and lunges at him.

"Stop that, Charlie," Roger shouts.

In two swift steps, I pounce on the rowdy devil and grab him by the scruff of the neck. At seventeen pounds, he can easily be picked up. He doesn't bite me, but he does snap and growl, fixated as he is on his aggression. Once he realizes I have him in my grasp, like a mother dog grabs her pup, he stops thrashing. I hold him off the floor with my left hand and, with my right, usher Rex toward his room.

We have a barrier about two feet high that we place across the doorway leading from the hallway into the family room. We can tell where Rex is, and he can see over it, but neither of the dogs can touch the other across it. Roger shoves the barrier across the doorway with Rex on the opposite side of it, and I carry Charlie to the kitchen, plunk him down, and pull the gate across the entrance.

Fuming, I stomp over to the sofa and sit down. "What the heck was that all about?" I glare at the scruffy dog, who is now sitting on the tile floor.

"You ever notice he only acts like that when we're all in the same room?" Roger says.

I try to calm down enough to think about it. "You're right. When I'm here alone with them, they're very good dogs around each other. There are no evil eyes or growls of any kind."

"I also notice Charlie likes to be higher than Rex. When he sits on my lap or here on the arm of the chair, he towers over Rex."

"But he doesn't do any of that when I'm here alone with them during the day. He lies on that chair all the time, and Rex comes and goes throughout the house." I cross my legs and swing the top one. "I'm sorry to say it, but Charlie gets possessive when you're around, especially if Rex comes anywhere near you."

"He wants to dominate, to be top dog."

"He wants you all to himself." I uncross my legs and lean forward. "But Rex was here first."

"Doesn't matter. Charlie is feisty and stubborn."

"That's for sure."

"We'll have to watch them even more, and I'll be sure not to give either of them too much attention in front of the other," Roger says.

Again my hope for a harmonious relationship between the two dogs is dashed.

What the heck have we done? And what do we do with this young troublemaker?

My head tells me the big dog isn't a threat, but my hackles don't pay attention. Out there on the street, I had to fight for every morsel of food I found. Just the sight of Rex brings back those memories.

That day when I attack him, I don't mean to do it. It's just that I don't want to share. I want these people all to myself.

Female Peep puts me in the kitchen and takes Rex to his room, where I presume she gives him attention and love. Trouble is, I want love and attention like that from her too. I want to be petted and hugged and feel the warmth of her arms around me, but something is telling me not to trust that this is a forever home for me.

Maybe these peeps are going to give me back. They can still do that. Heck, I've given them plenty of reasons to want to return me.

After talking to Male Peep, Female Peep gets up from the couch, walks over, and before she removes the gate, she says, "You have got to stop being aggressive with Rex, and you have to stop chasing your tail. It's not pretty. You're a better dog than that."

She thinks so? I can be a better dog than the one I am? I'd like to be.

Then I hear my name.

"Come here, Charlie Bear," Male Peep says.

I sprint the short distance from the kitchen to his recliner and leap into his arms. He holds me to his chest and pets me.

Ah, bliss. Why can't I get this same love from the Female Peep?

Chapter Nineteen

The next day I ask myself a tough question. *Should we keep this hardboiled, pushy, obstinate dog?* We're putting Rex at risk, which is not our intention, and it isn't fair to him. It will be tough, but we can admit to Sara and Ryo we were wrong, that this dog has issues we can't handle. Charlie needs more training and maybe even visits with that trainer he worked with before. We've been so busy, I haven't had the chance to look into it.

The bottom line: this scrapper's behavior is unacceptable. What the heck is going on with him? I understand it takes time to change, but this is not going to work. And who is in charge anyway? This pigheaded little rascal, though insanely cute, is not the boss. If I can't get Charlie to tow the line, he'll have to go. That's that.

Then a second thought creeps in, a niggling feeling. Something tells me not to give up on him.

Not yet.

What that feeling is, I don't know. Call it gut intuition, or call it a nudge from God, but I want to fight it. It would be easier to go back to the way we were: Roger, Rex, and me.

But in my mind, I hear a silent plea beseeching me to give this dog one more chance.

I lead Rex outside and let Charlie follow me into the garage. Then I shut the side door. "Listen up, buster. You are not in charge around here." At one-quarter the size of Rex, it's unbelievable how Charlie can even think he can dominate.

Charlie stares up at me with that impish face and then sits down. "Don't give me that adorable look. You're a willful bugger."

One of the many cupboards in the garage contains cleaning supplies for the cars, windows, and countertops. I find an empty bottle with a trigger top, sniff inside to be sure it hasn't contained any other liquid, rinse it, and fill it with water.

"Okay, here you go. This is a squirt bottle." I brandish the clear plastic bottle with the red top in front of Charlie. "You are going to get squirted whenever you do anything you are not supposed to do. If you scratch the screen door, growl at Rex, or go into one of your spin cycles, you will get squirted." The tone of my voice surprises me. It's strong, forceful, angry—and hopeful.

Why does it take me so long to remember things? I had one of these ten years ago when Rex was a puppy, and he learned fast. Even though Rex loves water, the squirts startled him and redirected his attention away from whatever he was doing. I'm hopeful it will work with this persistent guy. I turn the nozzle to the jet stream setting so the water shoots the farthest when I pull the trigger.

I'll try anything to get this dog to behave. I do want to keep him. He loves Roger, and Roger loves him, but pouncing on Rex is not winning Charlie any points with me.

A day later, I get the chance to try it out. Charlie is getting a little too exuberant with the pillows on the family room sofa. For some reason, he likes to bite them and grab them with his teeth. They're light but almost as big as he is, and it's comical to see him grab one with his teeth, toss it off the sofa, pounce on it, and then bite it over and over. I find him on the floor with one of the pillows in his mouth. He growls with each shake.

I grab the bottle and squirt. The water hits him on his left shoulder, and he drops the pillow. Then he mauls the pillow again. I squirt again, and this time, he snarls at the stream of water.

"Charlie," I say kindly, "get used to it. We're starting tough love around here, and you have to learn the rules."

I walk over, pick up the pillow from the floor and place it back on the sofa. When he first moved in with us and bit the pillows, I put them in the hall closet. But a couple of weeks later, I wondered why I did that. Sure, you'd baby-proof a house, and you'd even puppy-proof a house to keep puppies away from things that might hurt them. That I did, of course, but pillows are not going to harm him. And I should not have to rearrange the furnishings or decorations.

"Besides," I add to Charlie as he looks up at me, "the water won't hurt you; it'll show you when you're over the line."

I saunter past him with a nonchalant attitude and keep the water bottle nearby on the coffee table.

Our rainy season spans a few short months in the early part of the year. We don't normally get torrential rain, so one day, hoping it will slow to a drizzle or a mist, I wait to bring the dogs outside. But it's still falling heavily.

"There's nothing we can do but go out into it, guys." I snap open an umbrella and lead the way. Rex holds his head high and walks straight to the side of the yard. Charlie gingerly places one foot in front of the other and follows with hesitation, his eyes half shut and squinted, his body cowering from the pelting raindrops.

Halfway to the yard, he stops. "Come on, Charlie. Let's go," I cajole.

Rex finishes and stands on the patio, head lifted to the heavens. Sometimes he'll stand out there for five or ten minutes and let the rain fall onto his face. Charlie is having none of it.

I lead them both back into the garage. They're soaking wet.

"Let's get you both dry."

I grab two large, old towels and go for Rex first. His wash-and-wear coat repels the water well, but he still needs a vigorous drying. He stands still while I rub him from head to toe, and then he shakes his strong frame, and he's done.

"Charlie, your turn."

His fur, plastered to his little body, needs to be fluffed. I drape the towel around him and begin to rub. And he begins to growl.

"Stop that, Charlie Bear. You need to be dried."

I should have had a clue about Charlie not liking water by his reaction to the squirt bottle. And he doesn't like being rubbed with the towel.

Starting with his front end, I manage to rub his face, his front legs, and about half of his body from his nose to his rear.

"Shake, shake, shake," I sing to him in a lilting voice when I drop the towel for a break. I try to get him to believe this is a fun experience, and that a little rain won't hurt him. But more important, he needs to know that towel drying is a necessary part of life.

Charlie shakes, not because I sing to him in my off-key tone, but because of instinct. When Charlie shakes vigorously, his entire body lifts off the floor. I smile. "You're a cute little bugger."

I pick up the towel again. "Okay, we're getting there. But you can't go inside until you're drier than that." I take the towel to the rear half of him, and his growls intensify. I return to the front half and rub him a bit more; then I try to do his rear legs a little. More growls. Anywhere near his rear end is a definite no-no. He snaps at me.

"Charlie, this is not debatable. Look at Rex. He doesn't put up a fuss." Rex stands a few feet away and licks a front paw, his short coat almost dry.

"I swear you have hair and not fur, you little monkey. Look how long it is." It's stringy and stuck to Charlie all over. I try again to fluff him, but no luck. "Okay, you have to stay in the garage until you dry."

I take Rex to his room and go into the garage to play with Charlie a bit. I throw the ball for him so he'll run back and forth. Then I let him come in.

The next time they have to go out in the rain, I take a chicken treat and cut it up into tiny pieces. When I start the toweling process with Charlie, I lay down three or four pieces in front of him. His attention is focused on gobbling up the goodies and not on being fluffed and dried. After he eats those, I put down more and continue to work on drying him a little at a time. As long as there is something to eat, his focus remains on the food and not on snapping at the towel or at me.

Another eureka moment with this dog! He loves treats enough to forget about what is being done to him. Well, most of the time anyway. It isn't always easy, but it is a lot better.

CHAPTER TWENTY

LIFE BOILS DOWN TO increments. I flip the calendar to February and tick off the accomplishments. Another month of not smoking for Roger—check. Another month of halfway acceptable behavior for Charlie—check. Another month of keeping Rex safe—check.

What does Charlie Bear think about his new home? He has been with us about four months when I remember he'd been at his foster home for the same length of time. Is he testing us? Does he think this is when we'll give him back?

At this point in his history, he has been given away by his foster mom, who showered him with lots of love in spite of all of his issues. Charlie doesn't understand she groomed him for a forever home and she continues to love him, even from afar. All he knows is that he was taken to a new place with new people. Does he think now, after another four months, he'll be given to a new home again?

Maybe his behavior with us is a test to see if we are weak or strong. Will we give him up if he's too much trouble, or will we weather the storm and hope for sunshine someday?

The jury is still out.

We do begin to notice a few things Charlie does master.

After he shreds the screen—and I pay twenty-six dollars to replace it—he only needs a couple of squirts to get the picture. He now runs up to the door and stops short. His body quivers to be let out, but he doesn't paw at the screen. "Good boy, Charlie Bear," I praise. Another eureka moment.

In the beginning, when he ran those laps in the backyard (which we have come to accept as his way to expel energy), he barked at the two Jack Russell terriers that live next door. They climb to the highest spot in their yard, so they can look down at Rex and Charlie and then bark at them nonstop. We even buy one of those electronic bark stoppers we see advertised on television. We put it up in a tree and turn it on. It's supposed to work through sound frequencies. These dogs are unaffected and continue to bark. It drives us crazy to hear it, but there isn't anything we can do. The neighbors are often not home.

When Rex was young, right after the neighbors moved in, he barked back at the dogs. But we taught him to be silent, praising him when he walked around outside without uttering a peep. Now he ambles around the yard, oblivious to the cacophony. But Charlie takes up the call. I try to be vigilant about being near to our mouthy boy when he begins to bark, but often he's across the yard sounding off before I can grab the water bottle.

Gradually, we notice Charlie Bear begin to mimic Rex. Charlie zooms into the yard, races to the wall, runs laps, but he no longer verbalizes back to the dogs next door. Like Rex, he's learned to tolerate and ignore. Eureka again.

Watching Rex and Charlie together, I can't help but notice how different they are. At eighty pounds, Rex is muscular and solid. Charlie is a pipsqueak at only seventeen pounds with stubby little legs and a stocky body. He isn't a tiny thing, like those Yorkies we first looked at, but he doesn't have Rex's stature when he strolls around the yard.

There are other differences that stand out as well. Rex is a golden Lab, blessed with the temperament of a golden retriever and the short-haired coat of a Labrador. A good bath every couple of months is all his caramel-colored coat needs. He's prone to ear infections if he swims in a lake or a pool or if water gets into his ears during bath time. But I have medication to help to dry that up right away.

Charlie Bear's coat mystifies me. It isn't fur, at least not the kind of dog fur I'm used to. In some parts, it's curly like a poodle, and it doesn't shed like Rex's does. What confuses me even more is that it grows. If you snip a little of the length, it grows back. Rex never needs a trim, a haircut, or any kind of grooming beyond a brushing once in a while. Charlie needs it all.

And boy, am I surprised to find out a small dog has glands that need to be expressed. When I ask our vet about it, he says large dogs have the muscles to express the glands on their own, but a small dog often needs manual manipulation. I begin to notice Charlie throw those snarling fits and chase his tail when those glands are impacted. Well, I've learned another new thing about dogs.

So off to the groomer we go for a full-service bath that includes nail clipping, ear cleaning, and gland expression. Charlie doesn't like being fussed over, and he for sure doesn't like anyone messing with his rear end, so these groomer visits are not pleasant experiences. Sara told me her groomer would work with Charlie, give him treats, cajole him into allowing a little more grooming, and get as far as she could before she had to give up and give in.

I wasn't surprised to receive a phone call from the owner of the grooming spa where I'd taken Charlie that morning. "He's too matted and he's not cooperating. We've done all we can with him. Come and pick him up."

I sheepishly enter the salon where a young girl brings out a bewildered Charlie Bear. His ears droop, and his face looks sad. I'm sorry for what he has to go through.

Roger has been clipping Charlie's hair a little bit around his face. All of that fur grows and grows though, and we conclude a groomer visit once a month is a necessity.

But how do we get our lionheart to tolerate it? Neither Roger nor I want to put Charlie through the stress of it all.

"Let's work on him ourselves. We'll clip him and trim him," I say one evening after returning from that spa experience. "I'll feed him yummy treats while you snip out the matted areas."

"Okay, keep him occupied," Roger replies.

We snip and clip. Putting treats in front of Charlie's nose helps a lot.

But it's not until Charlie learns how to swim that we can really go to work on his matted fur. We've been wanting to teach him to swim, but that's impossible to do at our house in the winter. Our home came with a pool, as most homes out here do; but the winters aren't warm enough to swim unless it's heated, and that's too expensive.

But the swim lessons may not be able to wait much longer. After a couple months with us, Charlie Bear raced out the door as usual. But when he didn't make the turn on the concrete deck, he skidded straight into the pool. I dashed to his side and plucked him out, soaking wet and scared.

"Charlie, what the heck happened?" I pulled him close to me and took him inside. Later, I went out and put barriers around the pool.

Now, he'd dog paddled when he fell in, so we think he can swim, but we want to be sure. Rex often swims with us in the summer months, enjoying the throw of a knotted rope attached to a floating tube. He retrieves it in long strides as he paddles from one end of the pool to the other. It's good exercise, and we hope it helps with his arthritis.

We want Charlie to have the same happy experience in water.

Once in a while, we take a ride with the dogs out to Palm Desert, where we stay in a condo that has a community pool. The winters in Palm Desert are beautiful, and the community pool is heated. The rules state dogs aren't allowed in the enclosed pool area, but he's so little, I stick him under my arm and sneak him in when no one is around.

Charlie's heart beats rapidly the first time we place his tiny feet into the water, but we take it slow. "Here you go," I say in a soothing voice, "let's get you wet a little at a time." I hold him with my left hand and cup my right, bringing water up and over onto his back and his neck, and then a little on his face.

Roger wades out five feet, and when Charlie is ready, I encourage him to swim to Roger. Charlie paddles his little legs and swims straight to him. Roger turns him around, and Charlie swims back to me. "Good boy, Charlie. Good boy." We do the same thing a couple more times, and as serendipity would have it, Charlie does fantastically.

After a couple of visits to that pool over the next few weeks, we bring along our little clipping scissors. After the water bug swims a bit, he lies down on his towel and rolls over onto his back. He's tuckered out and malleable, a perfect time to snip those hard-to-reach mats on the underside of his body and on his rear legs. I go to work and soon have the mats clipped out.

Roger continues to work on Charlie, and finally, we have all of his matted fur removed. He looks a little scrappy, with hunks cut out here and there, but it'll grow back. We keep up a regimen of daily brushing, and on the next visit to the groomer, Charlie receives high praise from the young girl who works on him.

"He did such a good job," she says. "He tolerated the procedure so well this time. Congrats to you and your husband for working with him. It was a much nicer experience for Charlie Bear today."

Charlie's fur keeps growing back thick and lush, but we continue to watch for mats and take care of them as fast as we can so the grooming visits are not fear-filled experiences for Charlie.

We think all the attention to his body makes him more tolerant of being touched. I worried about whether he'd ever get over that, but he now has fewer growling episodes when he's towel dried, which is a relief. He even allows me to pet him and hold him for short stints. And when I walk past him, I fluff the fur on top of his head or run my hand down one of his sides. I try to tell him often that he's a good boy. Even if he isn't all the time, he does have good moments, so I praise him when I can.

The car rides out to Palm Desert can last an hour and three-quarters or, depending on traffic, a full two hours or more. Rex used to have the entire backseat of the SUV to himself for these rides. However, getting Rex into the car has become an issue in the past couple of years.

The day he tore his ACL will forever be a painful memory for me.

In the fall of 2008, I took him for a short car ride to a trail nearby. I had a regular sedan with four doors, and he easily jumped up and down from the backseat. We walked along the sandy trail where Rex sniffed and explored each inch. After a long stroll, we approached the trail end, and that was when it happened.

Rex was off to the side in the sandy area where some weeds grow when I heard him yelp. Instantly, he raised his rear left leg in the air. I ran to him and looked around. Had something bitten him? Had he twisted his leg in a hole? I didn't see anything that could cause him such distress. I looked at him closely. He had that look in his eyes. He was in pain.

Rex hobbled on three legs to the car, which was only a few paces away, thankfully. I opened the rear door in a hurry. He jumped in and huddled deep into the seat. Had he twisted his foot or hurt his hip? At that point, he often limped from his arthritis. Had the walk been too long? Had I pushed him too far in order to keep him active and well-exercised?

Once home, I kept a close eye on him, gave him a couple of aspirin, and waited to see if the injury would resolve itself.

It didn't, so we went to the vet, where he was diagnosed with a torn ACL. Surgery would be required to fix it.

The whole left rear quadrant of his body was shaved, and the row of stitches ran eight inches long. Rex didn't like the restrictions to his activity or the cone he had to wear.

"Come here, Rex. Let's take that thing off for a while." The Velcro made a ripping sound when I peeled one side from the other. "That'll give you a break for a while, huh, sweetie?" As long as Rex stayed in the office with me, I could keep an eye on him.

I rubbed behind his ears. I was so sad it had happened. It hurt to see him uncomfortable; his eyes were glassy from the sedatives and the pain pills. I kissed his soft muzzle. "You'll be better soon," I told him.

We nursed him through the long months of recuperation. We kept him restricted to one room of the house so he would stay off the leg as much as possible. He had no access to furniture, and he had to wear the protective cone until the stitches came out at six to eight weeks post-operation. There was to be no running or jumping for sixteen weeks.

Using the bellyband the surgeon provided to be sure he didn't fall, I walked next to him from the office to the yard for potty breaks. Then we walked back to the office again, where he melted down onto his cushy bed and closed his eyes to sleep. I stroked his soft fur thinking, *If only there'd been some way to keep this from happening.* The vet said big dogs are prone to this type of accident; still, I would've liked to have kept him from suffering.

It took more than nine months for his fur to grow in, which astounded the vet. He said Rex must have been quite traumatized from the whole thing.

Ever since that operation, Rex doesn't run and jump quite so much anymore, but he loves to take road trips. And we're overjoyed to have both dogs with us whenever we can.

Rex has been a good traveler since puppyhood. He sits in the backseat and looks out the window or lies down and sleeps. Well, he does bark if he notices a dog as we pass by, and I like to think that's his way of saying, "Hey, look at me. I'm getting a ride!"

He was eight and a half when he tore his ACL. Right after, we bought a telescoping ramp with a nonskid surface for the SUV. The specialist that Rex visited said, after one torn ACL, the other leg often becomes injured as well. We remain determined not to let that happen, so we continue to lead Rex up the ramp and into the car. He gets so excited that sometimes he approaches the back of the car and, even though I'm holding him on leash and straining to keep him away, he doesn't walk up the ramp. He prefers to jump up into the car before either of us can stop him.

"Rex, don't do that," I admonish. "You're going to hurt yourself."

When Charlie joins us, we're leery of allowing him to share the backseat with Rex. Charlie is too rambunctious, and we're bothered by his ambushes on Rex, so Charlie travels in his car carrier. This gives Rex two-thirds of the backseat, which is enough for him to stretch out and sleep. Charlie likes to be in his crate and often sleeps the entire way as well. Once we're out of the neighborhood and away from the sight of other dogs, we don't hear a sound from them.

"Maybe things are going to work out okay," I muse out loud on one of our rides in the car. I look over at Roger as he drives and then glance at both of the dogs. "Maybe Charlie Bear settled in, and maybe he'll be a good boy now."

Suddenly, Charlie lets loose with a piercing bark.

"What the heck is that for?" Roger asks.

"Not sure, but he's looking at Rex through the little holes in the side of his crate."

Settle in and become a good boy?

Then again, maybe not.

A few miles down the road, I look back. Rex is asleep. Charlie is quiet in his crate; his head rests on his two front paws. The rest of the ride is peaceful.

What I like to do most when I first get here is chew. Foster Mom brings a little bone with me, and I give that a vigorous gnawing. Female Peep buys me new toys, like this lime-green dragon thing with a squeaker in it. I also get furry animals for Christmas, and Rex doesn't mind that I play with his green banana. I do love that toy—it's the perfect size for me.

But sometimes, there are other things that entice me.

Like reading glasses—I like the black plastic ends. And Male Peep has a few wooden ducks from when he was in the Duck Hunters Club or something. The wooden, beady-eyed creatures sit around on the carpet in the family room and stare at me. So one day, I decide to bite their beaks off. I try and try, but the best I can do is leave little piles of splinters everywhere.

There are other items I take a fancy to—a little pair of scissors, the remote control, slippers, sandals, an emery board.

But what I love the absolute most, if you can believe it, is post-it notes. The little ones in a pad. They're up on *top of the desk in the office, just sitting there. There's a sofa near the desk, and it's easy to jump from one to the other. So I hop up there, grab the post-it notes, dash back into the family room, toss them up in the air, catch them, and toss them again. By the time anyone nabs me, those post-it notes are gooey history.*

CHAPTER TWENTY-ONE

"CHARLIE! WHAT DID YOU do to my books?"

Sitting in my office one afternoon, I glance at my bookshelf. As tall as I am and about five feet wide, it has four tiers loaded with all my stuff: a printer, a copy machine, accordion files filled with projects, three-ring binders, framed photographs, and lots of books. Charlie has not exhibited any interest in any of the things around the floor or bottom tier of my office so I think I'm safe in keeping items as they are.

I'm wrong.

I see he's chosen three of my hardcover books to gnaw on: *For One More Day* by Mitch Albom, one of my favorite authors; *A Dog Named Christmas* by Greg Kinkaid; and the book right next to that one, *Christmas with Tucker*, also by Greg Kinkaid. The spines and tops closest to the edge of the shelf are now a slobbery mess, and when I try to open the pages, they stick together. *Man, why'd he chew on the hardcovers and not the paperbacks?*

"Charlie, what's up with this?" Of course, it's my own fault. The past few years with Rex have lulled me into a false sense of security. Except for bread. That's never been secure or out of Rex's reach. He loves to snatch a loaf of crusty French bread off the kitchen counter, buns waiting to be toasted on the outdoor grill, or any sandwich left unattended on the table. He gobbles these things up in one lunging, yawning bite. But with anything other than bread, Rex has become a dog we can trust.

Charlie is small and can't lurch his body up to the countertop to grab food or reach the side table on the grill, but at eighteen months in age, he's full of steam and overdrive, like Rex was at that age. He has the same degree of high energy and insatiable desire to gnaw, chew, run, and play. When Rex was young, I thought it was because of his breed, but now I believe it's more because of age. I think about the many outings with Rex to the dog beach, the dog park, and the doggie day care. I also remember long walks and exuberant playtime in the yard.

When Roger and I were first married, we did a lot of things we don't do now. We stayed up longer, went out more often, entertained friends, and traveled a lot. Now, we often go to bed by 9:30, don't go out much at all, still entertain a bit (but not as much as before), and are content to travel less and stay closer to home. Life has changed, and Rex aged and changed with us.

Charlie is a young whippersnapper with a gung-ho enthusiasm for life. We can relate; but like we do when we party too much and regret it the next day, Charlie sometimes finds himself the victim of his own overzealousness.

One night, after a long walk with me, he runs around the perimeter of the yard like a madman. Rex puts himself to bed at half past seven, and it's time for Charlie to go into his den and sleep. But instead, he spins, snaps, and snarls at his tail.

"You know what?" I say to Roger while we consider Charlie's current problem. "He's overtired. He's throwing a temper tantrum, like a toddler."

We both laugh at the absurdity of Charlie's behavior. But we both understand. He's had too much of a good thing.

It soon becomes apparent whose dog this is. Of course, it has been evident from the very first day when Roger and Charlie Bear bonded in the backyard. But now, it's like an exclamation point has been added. I'm around most of the day; I feed Charlie, let him in and out, and give him treats at night when he goes to bed, but who does he run to for love? His main squeeze, Roger.

Roger lets Charlie Bear lie on his chest when he reclines in his chair. Charlie puts his paws up toward Roger's neck and then darts his little face forward to give Roger tiny licks and kisses. After a while, Charlie shifts his body to drape over the crook of Roger's left arm, hangs his face over the edge, and melts into the softness of the cushioned recliner.

In the afternoons, if I get home from work before Roger does, Charlie is the first to let me know Roger's truck is right around the corner. He hears it way before any normal creature ever could. He scurries to the hallway and crouches down. His tail wags and his body quivers. When the truck pulls into the driveway and stops, Charlie springs up. His small body squirms and squeals with pleasure.

"Daddy's home, Charlie Bear!" I sing out, though there's no need to say it. Calling Roger dad or daddy is an affectionate endearment Roger has earned. It doesn't take long at all for me to see Charlie considers Roger his number one.

When Roger comes through the door, Charlie jumps up and down with exuberant excitement.

"He sure does love you. Look how crazy he gets. He does that when you get up in the morning and when you come home. You're definitely his papa."

Yup, Roger has the moniker of daddy, or papa, if you will. He loves Charlie Bear, and Charlie Bear loves him.

Mom's birthday rolls around in April. My inbox is crowded with e-mails from florists—automatic reminders I set up to be sure to get flowers delivered for her big day. She loved purple, so I always searched for an arrangement that contained something with lilacs, irises, or purple tea roses. This year, I send sweet thoughts to her in heaven for being a wonderful mom.

All the "firsts" are difficult when you lose a loved one. For me, it's the first Wednesday I'd normally call her as I walk the dogs, the first birthday without her, the first summer vacation when she isn't there, the first Thanksgiving that I make her favorite recipes, and the first Christmas when I don't send her a card. I take a stab at making new memories to layer on top of the old. I'll never forget the memories I already have, but I consider adding a new chapter, one filled with acceptance and joy in spite of not having her here.

I realize this is the same way we try to handle Charlie Bear and his adaptation to our world. At first, there are so many new things, "firsts," for Charlie: a new home, new people, a new, big dog, and a new routine on top of it all. Stubbornly but successfully, he conforms to a lot of it, and we learn it's better to take things slow with him and to be patient and understanding.

As the months progress, Roger continues to stay away from smoking. I am so darn proud of him and his determination, though I think Charlie helps a lot.

It isn't always easy on Roger; the side effects of quitting are tough. Using my laptop, we often review the information about what Roger's body is going through. At first, he experiences lethargy, a common side effect of not having nicotine in his system.

"Feeling extremely tired is common, Roger," I tell him in the first few months. "Why not sleep in a little longer on the weekends? All the comments from people who have quit smoking indicate it eventually subsides."

Then there's a cough. It concerns me when I hear it, and I wonder why he's coughing now that he quit smoking. I google it and print out pages of information for Roger to read. We learn the hair-like cilia in his lungs, damaged from smoking, are now regenerating. "Your lungs are getting healthy by forming new tissue. Coughing is a common side effect. That will go away too." And it did.

Later it's irritability and inability to sleep. We cut out caffeine after dinner and give it time. To his credit, Roger stays the course. He takes it one day at a time, one week at a time, and one month at a time, all the while building up to a healthier body.

CHAPTER TWENTY-TWO

ON ANOTHER ONE OF those rainy days, I throw a toy for Charlie in the garage. It's a two-inch, jingling wire ball I'd bought for the cats. Charlie runs to and fro, bouncing and bobbing up to me with the toy in his mouth. He's pretty good about letting me take it from him, and sometimes he even drops it in front of me.

I switch to a furry stuffed bear that I toss the length of the garage floor, and he likes that even better.

"A tired dog is a good dog, Charlie Bear." That's an adage I believe in. If a dog gets his exercise, playtime, attention, and love, he won't go looking for activities to occupy him, such as gnawing on my books. At least, I hope and believe that to be true, so I try my best to keep Charlie busy.

One night, I sit in my usual spot on the sofa across from Roger's recliner. We're watching something on TV when Charlie Bear jumps up on the couch, inches next to me, lies down, and stretches his body tight against my side.

"Look at him," I say in a voice that's all mushy with emotion. "That's what Red used to do."

It had been a habit for Red to snuggle beside me each evening. Once Red settled against me, I was held captive and couldn't move, but I loved every minute we shared together, only pulling myself away when it was time to go to bed. Often, Red stayed in that same spot until morning.

It's funny to see Charlie Bear nestled by my side. Maybe he senses my sadness about my mom's passing.

A few days later, I'm at the computer reading e-mail and checking Facebook, when I hear the *click, click* of Charlie's nails on the tile floor. He sits down at the side of my chair, looks up at me with those sweet eyes, and wags his tail.

"What's up, Charlie Bear?" I stop typing, reach over, and heft him onto my lap. I put my arms around him and continue typing. He sits there, perched tall, and watches my fingers tap the keyboard.

A few minutes later, he turns his head and makes a move to get down. Swiveling my chair, I let him jump to the tile and he scampers out of the office.

"Huh, that was another first," I mumble.

It felt nice having his soft, warm, furry body close to me and his small head right underneath my chin.

One day Female Peep has an announcement to make. She looks joyful, so I'm not overly concerned, but you never know with her.

"Today is the six-month mark for Charlie Bear," Female Peep says.

"It's been six whole months?" Dad replies.

"Yup, time flies. I'd say he's steadily progressing to be a pretty good dog in the house."

Pretty good? She doesn't give me much credit. Lately, I have had very few spinning cycles; I don't guard my food or bones anymore because I know now they aren't going anywhere; and rarely do I let Rex, the big dog, get under my skin. I do follow him around a lot. The weird thing is, he teaches me stuff. I figure, because he's been here so long, there might be things I can learn from him, and I have.

"Charlie Bear," Dad says with a glad voice. "You made it to six months."

I jump onto his lap, and he pets me. I lick his hand.

"He started out at as a headstrong, bullheaded, seventeen-pound rascal, didn't he?" Female Peep adds.

"That's for sure."

I think I found my forever home here with Dad, Female Peep, and big dog, Rex.

What I forget to count on is how things can change.

Chapter Twenty-Three

In the month of May, right around the seven-month mark of Charlie being with us, Rex begins to slow down considerably. He leaves more food in his bowl than he eats, and sometimes Charlie gets out the back and sneaks around through the garage side door. I find him munching away in Rex's stainless steel bowl while Rex lies there and watches him.

"Charlie, you've had your food." I scoop up the bowl and shoo Charlie outside.

"Rex, what's going on? Don't you want to eat?" He looks at me with those big, brown, doe eyes rimmed with what looks like black mascara. I move the bowl right in front of him. From his prone position, he picks out a couple of nuggets and chews them. He appears to do it for me though, not because he's hungry.

"Rex, you've got to eat. Is it an upset tummy?" I scratch behind his ears and touch his nose. It's wet and slightly cold.

We all have days when we're not very hungry. I don't want to make it into a big deal.

A couple of days later, I see him slink out to the corner of the yard and throw up everything he's just eaten. I dash out to be sure he's okay, and he bounces across the yard, with a spring in his step, when I call out his name. Does he have a bug or something, like when we get the flu? Maybe that's all it is.

But Rex begins to vomit off and on. He keeps things down for a few days but then throws up again. What the heck is going on? Is it his food? I haven't changed it. His treats? Nothing different there either. Has he eaten something in the yard that would make him sick? I don't think so.

I watch him closely, and whenever I think it's time to take him to the vet, he seems to be better. But one morning, after he has all kinds of problems with vomiting and diarrhea, Roger and I take a hard look at him and realize he's getting skinny. I can see the outline of his ribs. It's strange how that creeps up on you.

I think about the last time I took Rex to the vet.

It was the first week of October, right after Red died. I wanted to be sure I was doing all I could for Rex because my fear of losing him was palpable and intense. At that visit, I queried Dr. Love about Rex's worsening arthritis and about the thyroid pills he'd been taking for four years. "Is there anything I can do to help Rex along as he ages?"

Dr. Love looked in his chart. "We've had him on aspirin to help with the arthritis." He looked at me kindly. "You're doing all the right things."

"But am I doing enough?"

This big sweetness of a dog is my everything. I can't stand it if he's hurting or if there's something I can do to take away the pain.

"Rex will probably only make it to eleven or twelve—" Dr. Love continued.

My eyes sprang open, and I tried to swallow my shock.

"This is due to his breed, size, and health issues." Dr. Love stopped moving the stethoscope across Rex's chest and looked up at me. He stood up fast and added, "Maybe twelve or thirteen."

At that point, Rex's eleventh birthday was three months away.

Now, I'm not ready to even think about losing my best buddy—not now, not so soon—not ever.

I place the ramp at the back end of my small SUV and lead Rex up and into the car. He likes to sit in the backseat with the window down a little ways, his face turned toward the breeze. Today though, Rex doesn't sit up on the seat. Instead, he lies down in the cargo area, his head on his paws.

As we drive to the vet's office, I glance often at him and say some prayers.

It's a sunny, bright day in May, the kind of day when he'd romp at the dog park in his younger days. This weather reminds me of when we'd take a jaunt through the neighborhood or a leisurely walk to his favorite spot by the wetlands.

Dr. Love conducts a thorough examination.

"Has he been eating?" he asks.

"Yes, but then he throws it up right away."

"Is he drinking water?"

"Not excessively."

"Are you trying a different kind of food? Did he get into anything he shouldn't have eaten?"

"I don't think so, and he's on the same food as before."

Dr. Love palpates his stomach, listens with his stethoscope, checks his temperature.

"We can do an X-ray to rule out anything that might show up on the film." He stands up and looks at Rex. "His sudden weight loss worries me. He needs to get some weight back on as fast as possible."

"I have him on a healthy dry food for weight control."

"Now's the time to give him anything he'll eat. And I'm sending you home with pills he needs to take three times a day and medication to add to his food."

There isn't a clear-cut reason for Rex's constant vomiting, and the X-ray doesn't indicate anything. Even though I wanted one, there's no definitive explanation or prognosis. Dr. Love suspects a couple of things, but invasive testing would be required to find out more.

I don't want Rex to undergo any painful procedures. He's been through so much with his latest surgery six months ago to remove a growth on his head and a hanging, problematic growth underneath his earflap. They were minor things, and in hindsight, I shouldn't have worried about taking care of them; Rex had to wear the cone around his neck so he couldn't scratch at the stitches. Watching him with that hang-dog look of having to endure the cone made me sad. I don't want to add to his discomfort.

We hope the medicine will help him want to eat. If he can keep food down, he can put on some weight and start to get better.

The problem is he doesn't get better.

"I'm extremely worried about him," I admit a few days later when Roger comes home from work. "What are we going to do? He won't take his pills, not even in a Pill Pocket."

"Not even in peanut butter?"

"Not even in peanut butter. If I make him take the pill, he throws it up."

The worry lines increase around both of our eyes and trepidation hits me like a punch in the stomach. I have to do something, but what? How can he not want peanut butter, his all-time favorite? I give him ice water and refill his bowl often. He does drink, but he won't eat.

The next day I call Emily. She's a vet tech. Other than Roger and me, she has spent the most time with Rex, taking good care of him when we're on vacation. I trust her as much as I trust Dr. Love.

Emily tells me she'll come over that afternoon after her time at the stables. She owns horses and boards them at an equestrian center not far from where we live. A little pixie of a woman, her compassion for all animals is huge. She's wearing casual riding clothes when she arrives; her short, cropped, blonde hair sticks out from underneath a baseball cap.

"Oh, sweet old man," she says, cuddling Rex's head. "What's going on with you?"

I explain the pills and the food I've tried.

"Get weight on him any way you can," she says. "This isn't the time to fret about proper food; you need to buy the juiciest, most appealing food you can find. Go for the bad stuff, the kind of canned food with lots of fat in it. That's what makes dogs love it so much."

"I've always given him the healthiest food I can because of his thyroid issue and his size. I don't want extra pounds to impact his already arthritic joints."

"You've always done the best for him. Now he needs you to switch gears. Give him all this stuff the vet has prescribed;

it's all good for him and won't hurt him. Extra treats are fine. Anything at all."

"He won't take the pills. He spits them out." I close my eyes for a moment and then open them and look at Emily. "I want to do more to help him."

"Just do your best," Emily says and hugs me and then Rex. "Get better, old man."

I rush right out and buy soft food in plastic packages, canned food that's rich in gravy and all sorts of yummy treats.

We try everything. At first, he gobbles up anything new, but then it comes right back up.

He's not keeping anything down.

Friends tell me it's a telltale sign the end is near when they stop eating their favorite things.

I don't want to believe it.

A few days later, after I try and try to get Rex to take the pills that are necessary and to eat something, anything, Roger comes home from work and asks, "How is he today? Did he eat?"

"I gave him some bread, and I made him a hamburger and hand-fed it to him. He's very listless." I wring my hands. "I'm very worried."

Rex limps along on bread, hamburger, and cooked chicken for a while, but he can't keep these things down. He loses fifteen pounds, going from eight-one to sixty-six.

It doesn't look good for him.

Chapter Twenty-Four

The days seem to crawl by in slow motion, and yet in other ways, the hands on the clock race too fast. I brush my teeth in the morning, even run a comb through my hair, but I don't wear makeup. There's no use putting it on when it all comes off in a blubbering mess. I blow my nose constantly, which turns it red and raw. My eyes are bloodshot and swollen from crying. This is my baby we're talking about here. I love Rex as much as I love my children. The exceptional connection we've had for more than eleven years is deep and strong.

Rex is special to me. Really special. I've had many animals in my life: dogs, cats, rabbits, and hamsters. My sister even had a ferret, but I didn't like it much. I become most attached to dogs, like my dog, Bogie. He was my constant when life's variables happened, such as another move to a new house and a new school. Bogie and the other dogs in my life have been memorable, but none of them have ever been like Rex.

My connection with him is hard to describe. I look into his eyes and see the depth of emotion we share. I watch his frolicking bouncing at the beach and feel the joy he feels. I hear his blissful whine when we drive down the gravel driveway to Nancy's house and feel at peace because he loves doggie day care.

His pure adoration for me keeps me on cloud nine all the time. I never tire of his elated bark when the garage door goes up, signaling my arrival home. Nor do I go without noticing his tail wags upon greeting me or his big licking kisses.

A few times a year, I buy him stuffed animals from the swap meet. I pick out the cutest and softest ones and haggle with the sellers to get them down to a dollar. On a Saturday morning, I sneak in a bag of three or four and pick out one at a time for him to play with. He carries the toy around all day long as his prize, his possession. He's an exuberant, cheerful dog. A day or two later, he tears into the stuffed toy, first going after the eyes because they're crunchy, I guess. He yanks them out and spits them to the side.

Then he rips open a stretch and methodically pulls out the stuffing. He then spits that to the side and shakes the carcass back and forth. The family room is littered with white, cotton batting, reminding me of a snow-filled landscape in Wisconsin. Lying with his paws over the top of his now-unstuffed toy, he'll watch me pick up the piles of white and discard them into a wastebasket.

"Good job, Rex," I tell him. I swear he grins.

He brings me joy, laughter, and happiness. The thought of losing him is unbearable. Why, oh, why, do I have to say good-bye again? Isn't it enough that Diamond left, and then Red, and then even Mom? Does Rex have to go too?

Life seems unfair. Cruel. Why can't our loved ones be around forever? Why do they have to leave? I hate this part. I hate saying good-bye. With Red and Diamond, I knew they were in pain. Even Diamond exhibited symptoms of some kind of illness before she had her stroke and died during the night. We figured Red would go first because he had so many issues with his diabetes. But she went first, and six months later, he followed.

A couple months after that, Mom was gone. It wasn't in an instant or something unexpected. Nonetheless, it was a shock.

Are we ever ready to see a loved one go? Especially a mom or dad? I wasn't. Yet I knew it was coming. She'd been sick for years and very sick for months. The doctors warned us her congestive heart failure, or complications from it, would one day take her life, and that's what happened.

I knew it was coming, and I tried to be prepared. I went there more often to see her. I sent her more cards just to say, "I love you." I called, and we talked for hours. But now, months later, there are moments when I wonder if I could have done more.

Now Rex is sick. Profoundly sick.

Will I lose him too?

Chapter Twenty-Five

Over the course of more than a week, I go through the motions. I make meals and phone calls. I go to work a little but keep my sunglasses on. I wear no makeup, no mascara. I live with red-rimmed eyes and no sleep. Life swirls around me, but I have only one thing on my mind.

Fearful Rex will succumb during the night, I tiptoe down the stairs numerous times, past Charlie Bear in his crate. Each time, Charlie opens his eyes but doesn't lift his head. "Go back to sleep, Charlie," I whisper. "I'm only checking in on Rex again."

I creak open the door to Rex's room and look inside. As soon as I see his side heave with a breath, I know he's okay for a while. Shutting the door as softly as I can, I walk past Charlie, climb the stairs and ease into bed. Tears spring fresh to my eyes and drip down to my pillow that's already wet.

I will not give up. I wrack my brain to think of anything at all that Rex might eat. There's a food I haven't tried. Saltine crackers.

When I was a little girl and I was sick, Mom would walk into my room with a metal tray with scalloped edges. It was adorned with flowers or a scene from a Norman Rockwell painting; I can't remember exactly, but I do remember the two small, fold-open legs underneath. It was the bedside tray, and if we were stuck inside and couldn't go out to play, she'd put a box of crayons on top and a brand-new coloring book.

At lunchtime, she'd take the tray into the kitchen and return with a bright napkin laid on it, a small plate of saltine crackers in the middle, and a glass of Seven-Up.

"This will help you feel better," she always said, and it almost always did. Within a matter of hours, my tummy ache was soothed, and I went out to play.

Rex won't eat his beloved peanut butter, but maybe he'll like some on a saltine cracker. I grab the big, plastic jar of creamy Jif, a sleeve of saltines, the tub of butter, and a knife. I stand in the garage next to Rex and pull out one cracker at a time. I slather it with butter, smear it with a swath of peanut butter, and with tears streaming down my cheeks, I feed each one to Rex. I choke down one for every three or four he eats.

When the sleeve of crackers is gone, I kneel beside him and cup his face in my hands. I kiss his muzzle and gently pet his soft, silky fur. "I love you, Rex. I'll always love you."

I look into his eyes, now troubled and pleading. He trusts me to do what is right.

Chapter Twenty-Six

How do you decide when it's time? How do you know when you must do the right thing for your beloved pet?

Roger and I talk for hours each day. It's painful to consider that Rex is too sick to get better. I want to save him, make him well, and bring the joyful dog back into our lives that graced our home for more than eleven years.

I'm not ready to let him go. I want more time, more fun. I want to give him many more hugs and kisses.

But when do we know we've run out of time? Maybe the answer is in the question. Do we know the time is up when we start asking ourselves this very question?

We look at Rex together that morning and assess how he's doing. It isn't good.

"He doesn't want to live this way," Roger says. "And we don't want him to be in pain, right?"

A sigh escapes me before I answer. "That's what I keep thinking about. Remember when he tore his ACL? He yelped once when it happened and then didn't say a peep. He stoically stifled the pain and hobbled around on three legs for the longest time while he recuperated after the surgery."

Roger smiles at me. "Remember how we called him 'tripod dog?'"

"Yes, and I also remember how long it took him to get better. He was what, eight and a half? The sedation, the confinement, the curtailment of activity—he didn't like any of it."

"And we didn't like it either that he had to endure that."

"No, we didn't," I add and swipe at the tears on my face again.

"Dr. Love said he'd make it to eleven or twelve. He's halfway between."

I ball up a Kleenex in my hand. "It's not long enough. Why can't he live a long time, like to fourteen or fifteen, like some Labs do? Why does he have to go so young?"

Roger doesn't say anything.

"I'm not ready to say good-bye. I'm going to miss him so much."

"I will too."

We sit in the family room; Charlie Bear is on Roger's lap, seemingly oblivious to the scene unfolding in our household. Rex is lying on the carpet runner at the end of the sofa.

"We agree his quality of life has drastically reduced, right?"

I nod my head.

"We could do more tests and exploratory surgery. But if Dr. Love finds something, how is he going to treat it? Would Rex have to stay in the hospital? Would he take the pills required to get better?" Roger's voice is low and quiet. "What if he has cancer?"

He's saying all the things I've been thinking. All of my fears now have a voice.

"At his age, would we want to put him through radiation or chemo? Would we want him to suffer or to be in pain?"

No. I want to shout no. But I say nothing. I can't. I'm torn, ripped in two. I want him to be better. But my desire won't cure him.

"Do you think he's trying to tell us it's his time?"

When Roger says those words, the dam breaks. I crumble and sob. I look into Rex's eyes. I know what he wants, what he needs. Am I strong enough to give it to him?

"Think about it, okay?" Roger makes a move to get up, and Charlie Bear leaps to the floor and then bounds to the back door. "What gets me is that Rex has slowed down so much in the past few years. He hasn't been the same since his ACL surgery. He doesn't play or romp much. He seems to go through the motions of life. I'm wondering if, for a dog like him, this has been a long and full life."

Roger pauses and then adds, "Maybe he's ready to go."

He walks over and hugs me, lets me cry on his shoulder, and holds me a few inches away. "It's hard. But we have to do what's right for Rex."

I manage to squeak out, "You're right."

"I have to get to work. I'll call you later, okay?"

"Okay." I walk to the door and let Charlie outside. He sprints to the flagpole and runs his races. Full of energy. Full of life.

I turn away.

CHAPTER TWENTY-SEVEN

WHY DO I HAVE to do this again? Eight months ago, I wrote a letter to our vet about Red. I made an appointment to bring him in, but I knew myself and that once I started to cry, my throat would close up, and I wouldn't be able to talk. There was so much I wanted to say to Dr. Love and his staff about how I appreciated all the compassionate care they'd given Red over the years and throughout his battle with diabetes.

We brought Red every three months for glucose testing; during these appointments, he spent an entire morning being pricked with a needle every couple of hours. The tests determined how the insulin was working in his system and if we needed to increase or decrease his dosage. Over the years, his dosages had fluctuated. Each time though, the staff comforted him and told me what a good boy he was. Still, I hated to put him through the ordeal.

With tears streaming down my face, I sat at my computer and composed a short letter telling Dr. Love and the staff that I wanted to be in the room with Red when they put him to sleep. I felt I owed Red that he not be alone. I went on to say it would be very emotional for me, and I wouldn't be able to talk when I cried, so I was sending the letter to indicate how much I appreciated their heartfelt care.

October 1, 2010, was the date I put on the top of the letter. It was the day of Red's birthday into his life over the rainbow bridge. It's a hard decision to make, but he hadn't eaten a bite in three days. He was drinking water, but he'd been vomiting, like Rex has been doing. He appeared to be shutting down. At fifteen and a half we didn't want to prolong his life any longer; he'd put up a long, hard fight. When I looked into his glassy, milky eyes, I knew what we had to do.

Roger drove the car that morning, and I held Red, who was wrapped in a large, fluffy towel. He meowed a bit, like he always did on car rides, but I held him close and talked to him. "It's your birthday today, Red. You're going to see Diamond later."

We pulled into the parking lot. I carried Red inside and held him as the shot was administered. He went to sleep, and I knew he was in peace.

Roger drove us home, sad at the loss of Red but glad he was no longer in pain. Both Diamond and Red had lived long lives and given us much pleasure and joy. We'd miss Red in the house, but we knew he'd be with his beloved Diamond. Once again, they'd lick and caress each other and sleep curled up, side-by-side, with their arms entwined.

I hate the thought of its being Rex's turn. I don't want to do this. I don't want to make that ride to Dr. Love's office for anything other than a good visit. I want to curl into a ball, go back to bed, and make all of this go away.

But looking at Rex makes it real. He depends on me. All his life, he has been so strong and stoic. Now, he is counting on me to be strong and help him. I hold his face in my hands again and look into his eyes.

It's time.

I make a call to Julie, a close friend who's aware of my struggle.

"I love him too much to let him suffer." My voice cracks. "It's because I love him that I have to let him go."

She reassures me I'm doing the right thing. A few months prior, she'd made the ride with her older Lab for the same reason. "When they tell you with their eyes, you can sense it. You're doing what's right for him," she says.

I want that to comfort me, to make me feel better, but I cry even more.

Eight months to the day that we had to send Red over the rainbow bridge, I again write a letter to Dr. Love and his staff.

B. J. Taylor

June 1, 2011

To: Dr. Love and staff

From: B.J. Taylor

This is a hard decision to make, but it's with a heavy heart we tell you Rex is ready to go over the rainbow bridge. His eyes say it all. The last few days have been extremely bad. He's vomiting; he has diarrhea; and he has refused all food— even yummy treats. Ever since his operation two years ago, he hasn't been the same. We've talked about it in depth and feel his quality of life is no longer good. We're keeping him going with cooked chicken and hamburger, and he likes bread. He has always loved bread.

We could probably limp him along on that type of food for a while, but he won't take any pills at all. When I shove them down his throat, he vomits them back up. At his age, we don't want to put him through exhaustive tests only to give him a bit more time. We don't want him to suffer.

Just like with our cat Red, I want to be inside the room, holding and petting Rex when you put him to sleep. I owe it to him that he not be alone. I want you to know we appreciate all the care you and the staff have given him.

I can't talk when I cry—and I'm sure I'll be crying buckets—so I want you to know all this before we get there. Rex has always been a great dog, and we're going to miss him so much. This is going to be hard, but we're doing it because we love him.

Thank you,
B.J. and Roger Taylor

Something shifts in me, and it isn't only the atmosphere in our house for that long, long week. It's my feelings for Female Peep. She's taking care of Rex like he's her baby. Like a mommy cares for her young. She holds his face in her hands and kisses his muzzle. She pets his fur and whispers to him how much she loves him. She looks into his eyes and sees how much he trusts her to do what is right. As much as any person can love an animal, that is how she loves him.

And that's why it makes it so hard to do the next thing we all know she needs to do.

For big dogs, like golden Labs, everyone understands that making it to eleven or twelve is a pretty good life. Some beat the odds and make it to fourteen or even fifteen. Of course, we all hope we can be here forever. But the fact is, we can't.

To me, young rascal that I am, death and dying seem a long ways away. At first, I romp and play as usual that morning, but I feel the somber mood too. So I grab my stuffed squirrel and retreat to a corner of the sofa.

Right after lunchtime, Mom puts a collar and leash on Rex and says good-bye to me.

"I'll be home soon, Charlie Bear," she says. "Be a good boy."

And off she goes. She doesn't tell me it's the last time I'll see Rex, but that's okay. I know about the rainbow bridge. All dogs know about it; even cats know too. And I know I'll see Rex there someday.

Chapter Twenty-Eight

That morning Roger spends some alone time with Rex, saying his good-bye. He kisses me and gives Rex one final pat on the head. "I love you, Rex," he says, and then he turns to go, his own emotions bubbling over.

The appointment isn't until the afternoon. At twelve thirty, I pull my car out of the garage, put the ramp at the back and lead Rex up and inside. He lies down again, resting his head on his paws.

I tip the rearview mirror so I can see him on the ride to the vet's office. My big boy barely keeps his eyes open. Mine blur with tears. Traffic is light, thank God, so navigating the streets is easy, but it also means we pull into the parking lot more quickly.

The staff, compassion etched on their faces, indicate an open exam room door when I walk in with Rex. I hold his warm, soft blanket from home under my arm.

Inside the small room, the metal exam table is folded up against the wall and on the floor is a large heavy blanket. I lay the blanket I've brought on top of theirs. In red and blue letters, mine declares, "A mother's love is everlasting." I want them to wrap Rex in it after he goes to sleep. I want him to know I will always love him. Always.

Dr. Love enters, and his caring blue eyes meet mine.

"I got your letter," he says. "I understand. You're sure you want to do this?"

No! I want to take Rex to the car, go home and live many more years together. I compose myself enough to nod.

"Okay, I'm just checking. He's such a great dog," Dr. Love stands there, his six-foot four-inch frame towers above me. The guilt at that moment overwhelms me. *Am I doing the right thing? Am I rushing this decision?* Maybe it isn't Rex's time.

Dr. Love's compassionate face turns to me. "I suspect he has cancer," he says softly. "Without further tests, we can't be sure, but that's my speculation."

I nod.

"Here's what's going to happen. I'll administer the shot, which will enter his system pretty quickly. He'll close his eyes and go to sleep. It won't take long. I'll check his vitals to be sure he's gone, and then after, you can stay with him as long as you want. There's no rush, no hurry. Let yourself out when you want to go." He pauses. "Did someone come with you? Are you going to be okay to drive?"

I hug Rex hard and stammer, "I'm okay. I'll be okay. I drove, but I'll be okay."

"I'm worried about you driving. Sit in the parking lot for a while then, okay?"

"I will."

Dr. Love looks at both of us one more time and puts his hand on the doorknob. "I'll get my assistant, and we'll bring in the shot. Rex will need to lie down."

"He won't lie down. He doesn't do downs," I manage to say.

"Mike and I will take care of it."

I want to scream. They'll have to muscle him down, and I don't want that. Not on the day Rex will be going to doggie heaven. *Please God, not today.*

I caress Rex's head. He stands stock still, with a faraway look in his eyes. He doesn't like coming to the vet. He doesn't like these rooms. He's never even sat down on the floor. He stands looking at the door, waiting for the chance to get out. He'll let himself be examined when we have to do it, but he bounds out and heads for the car as soon as I open the door.

Even today, in his worn-out state, he stands, but he doesn't stare at the door. I hug him again, and then he does something he's never done in here before. He lowers his body onto the blanket. I look at him, not believing what I see. He lies there a good twenty or thirty seconds. I'm sure that as soon as Dr. Love returns to the room with Mike, Rex will leap up.

The door opens, and they come in. Rex remains on the blanket. It's incredible. He stays right there, lying down, while Mike puts his arms around his neck and Dr. Love searches for a vein in one of his front paws. I sit down beside Rex and hold his head in my hands.

Rex doesn't resist; he doesn't fuss. It seems to me like he wants this. Otherwise, why would he lie down, ready for them to take away his pain?

I whisper, "You're a good boy, Rex, a very good boy." He knows how much I love him; I don't have to say it again, but I do anyway. "Mom loves you, Rex."

Dr. Love injects the solution. In a matter of seconds, Rex's eyes close, and he seems to melt into the blanket. His head becomes heavy in my hands. Mike releases his grip and leaves the room.

I see a peaceful and serene expression on Rex's face as the slumber fills him. It's like watching my baby finally asleep and at peace. He's at rest now—no more pain or struggle.

After Dr. Love checks Rex's vitals, he lifts Rex and moves him to the middle of the blanket. Then he curls Rex's paws around his body. His head rests on his two front paws now, as if he's sound asleep at home. Dr. Love wraps my blanket around Rex and pulls it up to his neck, and then he leaves the room.

I kiss Rex and tell him how much I love him. "Say hi to Red and Diamond for me, okay?" I sit there for a few minutes, not wanting to say good-bye, and then I pet his head again. "I'll always love you, Rex. Always."

Rex's body, frail and sick, is all that is left. His spirit is free.

After one last look at my beloved, caramel-colored, sweet, gentle, loving boy, I get up and turn the handle on the door. There's no Rex to follow me out. No loving pet to jump into the car or sit on the seat sniffing the air from the open window.

I turn the key in the ignition, pull out of the parking lot and drive two blocks before I pull over.

I rest my arms on the steering wheel and my head on my arms. I close my eyes. After a while, I open my cell phone and call Roger. "Rex is at peace."

"Are you okay?"

"I'm parked at the curb by the vet's office."

"He's out of pain and up in heaven with Red and Diamond now."

"Yes." I wipe more tears from my eyes. "It was peaceful for Rex."

I tell him about it as traffic whizzes by; people come and go from errands and duties. Life crashes for a moment for Roger and me, but for others, it's business as usual.

"You're heading home then." Roger pauses. "Charlie Bear is waiting for you."

Charlie. The little rascal with the insatiable desire to play, romp, and challenge us with his antics and behavior.

Roger continues when he hears the silence. "We still have him."

"Yes, we still have him," I reply. But I can't tell Roger that this doesn't fill the hole in my heart. There will always be a special spot no other dog can fill. Nothing can ever replace Rex. Nothing will ever take his place. He's special and one of a kind. I will miss him forever.

"You did the right thing," Roger says.

Did I? Did we? Roger feels better saying those words, but I'm not sure I believe them. Not now. Not when I'm in so much pain.

"Be careful driving home, okay?"

"I will." I close the phone and try to convince myself we did do the right thing. It was Rex's time. But doubt creeps in. Maybe we made a hasty decision. Maybe we should have opted for more tests, an operation if he needed it, and treatment for whatever ailed him. We could have had him with us longer.

Yet, in my soul, I understand prolonging his time here wouldn't have been right. And didn't he give me the most sensational sign of all? Didn't he lie down on his blanket, enveloped in my love, at the end?

I pull out into traffic and drive home. Charlie Bear greets me with enthusiasm and his customary wiggle. He looks for Rex behind me, but when he doesn't see him, he runs, grabs his green turtle, and jumps up onto the couch.

This will take a while for all of us to process—Charlie Bear too.

Chapter Twenty-Nine

THE CLOCK READS 3:35 AM in bright red numerals when I'm startled awake.

"What is that?" I sit up in bed. It sounds like splashing, spraying, and dunking in the pool.

"Come here and look," Roger says.

He stands at the window, the blinds parted.

I throw back the covers and rush to his side. A loud noise breaks through the quiet of the night. *Quack, quack.* There are ducks in the pool. Over the years, we've had ducks fly into the pool, but it doesn't happen often. When it does, there are always two of them. One female and one male.

On the rare occasions when ducks have chosen our pool for a swim, they've swooped in silently and have barely made a splash to announce their presence. Sometimes, we haven't even noticed them until Rex has seen them. He'd rush up to the pool and bark, mystified as to why ducks would be in his yard, his domain, on his watch.

His barks never did any good. The ducks swam out of his reach. I loved to watch Rex's reaction when they spread their wings, took off, and flew away. His face registered amazement and awe, his eyes danced, and a tiny *woof* emerged from deep inside as he watched them disappear into the sky.

Ducks that land in our pool have always done the same thing; they glide around or sunbathe on the deck if Rex is in the house. But these ducks splash around and make a heck of a racket. And they do this in the middle of the night.

"Look," I comment almost in a whisper. "There are three of them."

We watch as one male and one female swim to the left side of the pool. They dive, dunk, and groom each other, and they seem to have a marvelous, rollicking, grand ol' time.

On the right is a stately, strong, sentinel male.

I know in an instant who they are, who they represent.

Diamond and Red, a female and a male, were best friends in their life here. They licked and groomed each other, played and frolicked through the house, and raced each other up and down the stairs.

When Red was quite young, around four or five, he broke his leg, probably from one of those forays up and down the steps at a hundred miles an hour. He never complained about the pain, and it wasn't until we noticed him hobbling a little that we had an X-ray taken. After surgery, he was good as new and home in Diamond's arms. They slept together, curled up in a ball, with their paws encircling each other. They hated to be apart.

Now here they are, together again.

And yesterday, our beautiful and beloved Rex joined them over the rainbow bridge. Rex loved to play with Red, but Diamond kept her distance and watched Rex from afar. One reason we had Rex sleep in his office was so we could close the door and allow the two cats the full run of the house at night.

Diamond waited on the staircase and watched Rex through the metal railing. She knew, right around seven thirty, Rex would go into his room and she could come down to the ground floor. She felt comfortable then, and she joined us in the family room for head and belly rubs, purring with contentment.

The lone, stately duck on the right side of the pool is my beautiful golden Lab. It's appropriate Rex is on that side, right outside the window of his office.

The three ducks make quite an announcement of their presence, and it surprises me Charlie Bear doesn't wake up or bark, though I'm sure he can hear them.

Roger and I stand mesmerized at the window.

"It's a sign," Roger says quietly.

"Yes," I barely breathe.

Quack, quack, the ducks announce. And it's almost as if I can hear the message they convey. *We're here to tell you we're all together, and everything is okay. Hey, Mom! Hey, Dad! We're fine. We're having fun. It's great here over the rainbow bridge. Don't worry.*

The two ducks on the left stick close to each other the whole time. They immerse themselves in the water, dunk their heads, come up, shake themselves a little bit—raising their bodies up halfway from the pool—and then they sink in again.

The beautiful, brightly colorful mallard on the right holds his head high and rigid and swims in tight circles. Confident. Proud. His quacks are pronounced, sharp, and loud, like Rex's barks used to be.

I smile. That's my boy, still comforting me, guiding me through this first night without him. Roger and I watch from the second-story window. Peace consumes our individual grief.

They quack a while longer, swim around a bit more, and then spread their wings and fly off into the night together.

"Wow," I whisper.

Roger reaches for me, wraps his arms around me, and holds me to his chest.

"That was so cool." I wipe away the tears and silently thank God for showing us His love for even the smallest of his creatures.

Our babies are okay. They're with each other.

The next morning, at six thirty, I sit at the desk in my office and look out the window. I'm there only a few minutes when a lone, male duck appears in the air on the far side of the yard, swoops low, and gracefully lands in the pool. I can't believe it. Another duck? By himself?

He swims on the right side, outside my window where I can see him bobbing. I used to watch Rex out this window on his many patrols around the yard.

The beautiful mallard sits in the pool for a long time. I can't take my eyes off of him. It has to be Rex again. After a while, he flaps his wings, raises himself up, and lands on the deck across from me. He sits there and looks straight at me. This is so unusual. It is extraordinary.

I can sense what Rex is trying to tell me.

I know you miss me. But it's okay. I'm fine. You did the right thing.

I watch incredulously as he stands there. I'm shocked but glad he visits me again. Then again, this is Rex we're talking about, and I think he sees I'm deep in mourning, second-guessing our decision, and missing him so much it physically hurts.

Then he begins to quack. *Quack, quack.* It's like he's talking to me. Roger is asleep. Charlie Bear is quiet in his crate. It's Rex and me together like always, every morning.

This is the first day I haven't opened the door to his room with one of my whispered greetings, "Rise and shine, sweetie," or "Are you up, sleepy head?" He loved to curl up on the sofa, but in recent years, his arthritis kept him from hoisting his body up there. He preferred to sleep curled up on his dog bed, a large, rectangular, cushy bed with paw prints and raised edges adorning the perimeter. I'm sure he didn't care what it looked like, but I liked him to have nice things.

Like the blanket and pillow in his room. I found them both in a dog magazine a number of years ago. The entire page of blanket throws caught my eye, but what I really zeroed in on was the one with the beautiful shade of soft blue and the short fringe around the edges. There was even a choice of dog breed in the center. There must have been a dozen or more dogs pictured.

Magazines usually have lots of merchandise depicting yellow Labs, light in color, almost white. But rarely do I see golden Labs. This time, there is one, a gorgeous, larger-than-life depiction of my beautiful Rex. The golden, sunshiny head of the Lab is offset by the darker, burned-caramel ears, the black-rimmed eyes, and the black, button nose. It's Rex to a T.

And on top of it, this company has matching pillows. I buy them both and use the blanket as a throw over the sofa. It's exactly the right size, and the pillow propped at the end becomes the perfect accompaniment. When I need a quick nap or to rest my eyes for a little while, I lie on the sofa with my head on the pillow and the blanket thrown over me.

The door to the office remained open during the night. Rex's dog bed stayed in its same location; the blanket and pillow are also still there on the small sofa. Everything is as I left it the day before, as if Rex were still here or coming home soon.

I sit at my desk now and watch the duck across from me.

His eyes never waver. They bore into me, trying to give me strength. This is going to be hard. I miss Rex so much. He's my baby, my boy.

He looks straight at me for more than half an hour. Then he flaps his wings and flies into the sky.

I think about heaven. I think about God.

Do I believe angels have wings? I most certainly do.

Chapter Thirty

CHARLIE BEAR IS ALONE in the house with Roger and me now. After the first few days of looking around for Rex, he seems to accept it.

I send an e-mail notifying friends and family Rex went over the rainbow bridge and how much it hurts to have him gone. One of my dearest friends responds with this quotation, "You never get used to losing them; you only get used to living without them."

Living without Rex is going to be hard, like it's hard to live without Diamond and Red. Time heals all wounds, the saying goes, and I agree with it to a point. It does heal, but the wound, at least for me, never fully closes. There's a part of my heart that yearns to pet them one more time, to cup their faces in my hands, to kiss their soft fur, and to snuggle them close.

Even the long ago losses of Bogie and Chumley, a dog I had in Wisconsin during the divorce from my first husband, never entirely healed. I even call Charlie Bear by the name Chumley a few times during the first couple of months Charlie is with us. The two dogs' sizes, statures, and attitudes mirror each other in many ways.

Chumley, a mixed breed, tricolor, scruffy dog—with a dash of border collie in him—was a little bit longer than Charlie is. He was wiry, independent, and sweet.

We found him at a junkyard, roaming in and out of the carcasses of abandoned and rusted automobiles. My first husband and I had driven to the yard to find a part for a car he was restoring. This little dog followed us up and down the rows and hung around near the entrance when we were ready to pay for our purchase.

"That'll be twenty-five dollars," the owner said in a gruff voice.

"That's a lot for this one part," my husband responded.

"That's the price. Take it or leave it."

All of a sudden I found myself chiming in. "We'll take it, if you throw in the dog."

"*Hmph*, got no use for him anyway," the man replied. He wore a pair of faded old jeans, a red and blue flannel shirt, and a battered pair of dirty, brown work boots. "You can have him."

My husband handed over two bills, a twenty and a five, and I scooped up the dog before the junkyard owner could change his mind.

"What's his name?" I asked when we got in the car.

"I called him Muttley."

We drove off with this new dog on my lap, a surprise junkyard purchase for me. I whispered in his ear, "That's not a nice name for a dog." Besides, he looked nothing like the animated cartoon character by the same name.

And to my husband—who was a little incredulous I'd negotiated for an animal along with his car part—I said, "How about we call him Chumley? That sounds like Muttley but cuter."

"Doesn't matter to me," he said and drove us home.

Chumley provided me with the comfort I needed years later during the heartbreak of that failed first marriage. After years and years of trying to make it work, it had come time for my first husband and me to part ways. That scruffy little dog was there for me, lying by my side, while I cried bowls of tears at the loss and insecurity.

Somehow, dogs seem to understand what you need and when you need it, just as Charlie Bear comforts Roger while he struggles through these months without smoking.

Now, many, many years later, the heartache of losing Chumley has never really gone away. And a new hole has been added to my heart with the loss of Rex.

CHAPTER THIRTY-ONE

THE FIRST WEEKEND IN June is noted on the calendar with the words "Nick's big day" and a giant, red heart. Our oldest grandson is graduating from high school in Wisconsin, and I've had a plane ticket in hand for months. Our youngest son is coming from Arizona to join the fun, and even my sister from Georgia plans to attend. It's a busy time of year for Roger at work, so he stays home with Charlie Bear. I'm looking forward to a few days away as a time to regroup. After all the tears and emotions, it'll be good for me to smile, laugh, and have fun.

After Nick's graduation ceremony at the high school, his mom hosts a party in the backyard at their home. We take pictures of Nick's black Lab, Oreo. He's a big dog, and he reminds me of Rex. I feel a tug of sadness. I snuggle Oreo's face next to mine and give him a kiss on the muzzle. Oreo is a young dog, full of energy, and he doesn't sit still long. Someone calls him, and he chases after a thrown tennis ball.

Nick entertains me with flips on the huge trampoline in the yard, while a roasted pig turns on a spit on the other side of the party tent. Salads, veggies, brownies and a huge cake are spread out on tables. We all eat our fill.

Later, Nick rides his motorcycle around the yard. Soon I hear, "Grandma, come on. I'll give you a ride."

I straddle the bike, being careful not to burn my leg on the muffler, like I did as a kid. The scar from that burn took years to fade. "Go slow, Nick," I tell him, which he does, but then he ramps it up a bit at the end. We zoom up to the crowd, and I grin with pride. That's my grandson, and what a fine boy he is.

For the next couple of nights, we rent rooms at the Brookfield Suites Hotel in Brookfield, Wisconsin, the same hotel where we gathered with Mom. It's bittersweet without her there, but I'm determined to make the best of it for the sake of the children. My brother and his kids join us.

The indoor pool becomes our personal playground when we find no one else in there one afternoon, and huge splashes from cannonballs spray my niece and her new baby. Nick and his brother, Colton, throw a football back and forth.

"Come in, Grandma," Colton shouts.

I peel off my cover-up and lower my one-piece-suited body into the tepid water. "Don't get me wet," I tell them.

"Yeah, right," Nick says, grinning, and then he splashes water right at me.

I grin and splash him back.

Hours later, the gang dries off, and we retreat up to one of the suites to watch a movie while the baby sleeps in her stroller. I think of Mom and how she lived for these annual events with all of her loved ones around her.

Evenings were her favorite because the front desk put out freshly made chocolate chip cookies. One night, Mom went to get a couple, but they were all gone.

"Shoot, did I miss them?" she said to the manager.

"We have another batch in the oven right now. Can I bring a couple to your room for you?"

"How nice of you," Mom said and smiled at him.

We turned her walker toward the elevator and shuffled down the long hallway to our room. No sooner had we settled in when we heard a knock on the door.

"Who is it?" Mom sang out.

"Your cookies, Ma'am," he replied.

Mom opened the door, and there he stood holding a plate of six warm cookies and three small, cardboard containers of cold milk.

On our last day at the hotel, my brother poses a question. "Are we going to keep doing this?"

"Do you want to?" I ask.

"Yeah, I do. The kids love it, and so do I."

"So let's keep doing it then—once a year."

"Good, okay. You came up this time because of Nick's graduation, but because Mom is gone I thought you might stop."

"I don't want to stop. Look how much fun we have."

"I love seeing you," my brother adds.

"I love seeing you too."

Over the next few months, Nick, Colton, and all my nieces and nephews e-mail or message me on Facebook. "When are we doing the hotel again?" they ask.

Life goes on, even without the loved one who has been an integral part. The children need it, and it's good not only for them, but also for me.

I make a promise to myself to keep the tradition going, and I talk to my brother, my sister, and my sons. We set the date.

The next reunion will be in July 2012.

When I return from that graduation weekend, friends point out the obvious. We still have Charlie Bear. They all mention how pleased we must be that we adopted him when we did. It's true that God must have orchestrated the timing because Charlie did fill a huge emptiness for my husband at least.

Roger had been missing Red so much, and that's when he brought up the subject of getting a new little dog. I, on the other hand, didn't need more than Rex. The heartache when we lost Red was almost too much for me to bear.

Here we are at the end of June now, and I've lost Mom and Rex. I do not want to open my heart any further to more heartbreak. I have to give Roger a lot of credit. He doesn't force me to open myself fully to Charlie; he allows me time to grieve. He grieves too, and his red, bloodshot eyes match mine again.

But Rex had been my dog. It may not sound fair or right, but it's natural for an animal to bond intensely with one other person or another animal. Rex and I were tight. Charlie Bear and Roger share a unique bond, even though they've only known each other for a short eight-month period.

I want to give my heart to Charlie Bear. He may be a spunky little monkey, but he's all we have left.

And yet for some reason, I can't.

I decide I have a job now, an important one. It's to bring smiles and laughter back to Mom and Dad.

It's not too hard with Dad. When he gets in his chair, I jump on top of him and snuggle in close. He smiles and pets me. He's an easy one. Like I've said, I've had him wrapped around my paws since I got here.

Mom Peep is, well, a bit tougher. She was always all about the big dog, and I can't blame her. Rex was a good dog. They both loved him a lot. I mean a whole lot. I only hope I can be that good of a dog one day.

So I'm working extra hard with Mom, and I can tell she's trying extra hard with me. When she grabs one of my toys and throws it from the family room into the kitchen, I run and chase it and bring it back to her. But I don't let her have it. We play the chase-and-grab game. She chases me and grabs for my toy. And I run around and around the coffee table, up and down onto the sofa, from the family room to the kitchen and back again. We play this "run around" game almost every morning. I hear her laugh one time when I stretch out all four paws and fly off the couch, "getting air" like in basketball. So I do that a lot.

We play ball outside now too. She kept the tennis balls hidden in the garage all those months because Rex, the big dog, was too old to play with them. He thought he could run and chase like he did when he was young, but his arthritis caused him to hobble if he exerted himself. Now, the scruffy, no-longer-yellow-but-still-good tennis balls come out. Boy, how I love the ball. I chase it, skid on the patio when I get close, and grab it in my mouth. Mom giggles if I miss and come up empty, but—sh!—she doesn't know I do that on purpose.

So life goes on at our house. It's a little different and much more somber. I try my best to put the fun back into life for them. And for me too. I'm a willful, pigheaded, mulish little mutt, but I'm loved. And so are they.

I plan on startling them once in a while with new tricks. I'm a whippersnapper of a dog with plenty of new ways to entertain them. I think they'll be surprised. Joyful love and abandon will again rule this roost. I know that will make Rex very happy.

And I've just got to say, for all the times I attacked Rex, for all the moments when I wished I was an only dog and had the peeps to myself, I have to admit I miss him.

Rex, you left big paws to fill.

CHAPTER THIRTY-TWO

OVER THE NEXT FEW weeks, we start to see some good changes in Charlie, such as a big reduction in the number of times he spins. He's down to a few per week now, and they seem to happen only when he's overtired or has too much stimulation. Charlie Bear is also more accustomed to my touch, and sometimes I take a mohair brush and run it along his chest or on the top of his back. He no longer guards his food or toys, and he readily allows me to put a treat down in front of him and then pick it back up, before I turn it over to him for good.

There are also things he learned from his buddy, Rex, like how to be a good sleeper. He has this pretty much down pat, with no fussing and no barking, but a week after Rex leaves, Roger raises a question.

"What do you think?" Roger asks one Saturday afternoon. "Should we let Charlie sleep in the office now?"

Charlie's large wire crate and carrier sit on a heavy blue blanket in our family room, shoved in between a small table and the fireplace because that's the only place it will fit. We want Charlie to have his own space, his own area he can go when he wants to be alone, but we want him to be near us as well. The wire crate is an imposing addition to the room, but it has been our only option until now.

Charlie often walks into his crate with a bone or a treat, so we realize he's comfortable there. And bedtime is easy now. He goes right to sleep without any fussing.

"*Hmm*, I don't know." I'm in the kitchen, and I look at Roger in the family room. "You mean put the wire crate and the carrier in there?"

"At first," he answers. "Maybe, eventually, he could sleep in there without them." Roger swivels his recliner to look my way.

"I'd want him to be comfortable." I stop ripping lettuce into salad bowls. "We don't want to give up the good routine he has going."

"Why don't we try it?"

"Okay, let's move the whole thing in and see how it goes."

We aren't too sure about Charlie having full run of the house at night, and we don't want to close the door to the room, so we bring out the flexible cardboard barrier. We used it with Rex to keep him inside the office when we wanted to be able to see in but didn't want him to get out.

We knew Rex, and Charlie too, could muscle through the cardboard or even jump over it, but neither of them ever have. It's more of a deterrent, and Rex taught Charlie to live by the rules. They didn't chew on it either. For all the years Rex could have jumped over gates, plowed through cardboard or plastic placed across doorways, he always respected the principle and never pushed the boundaries.

We lug the big wire crate into the office and put Charlie's carrier inside of that. Both doors are left open and he can come and go as he pleases inside the room.

The first night he roams around, a little out of sorts, but he relaxes and sleeps inside his crate. He's even better the next couple of days, so we remove the large wire crate and leave the small carrier, which we place on the large, cushy dog bed that belonged to Rex. The little carrier sits perfectly on one side.

"Let's add his round, fleece bed on top of the sofa," Roger says.

"And there's that square, suede, fleece-lined bed in the garage the cats never fell in love with. That's a perfect size for him. Why not put that in there too?" I add.

So in short order, Charlie Bear now has the office and the perks that go with it. And the open door, with the flexible barrier across the bottom, gives us the luxury of peeking in on him whenever we want to.

There isn't anything cuter than a slumbering child or pet, and Charlie gives us many reasons to smile when we see him curled up in his fleece bed. Sometimes we have to search for him and discover he's way at the back of his crate or in the deep square bed the cats never liked.

But the best part of Charlie's nighttime rituals, the one that makes us chuckle, is Charlie Bear's position on the sofa, tucked against the side arm.

"Come here. Look at him," Roger whispers, craning his neck around and peeking in.

"What's he doing?" I whisper.

"Look."

Charlie's four white legs stick straight up into the air, and his head and white-throated neck hang down off the end of the sofa.

"Have you ever seen a dog sleep like that?" Roger asks.

I stifle a giggle. "No, I haven't."

"That's unbelievable. How can he sleep in that position?"

"*Sh*," I whisper. "Don't wake him."

But you can stand right over him when he's like that, and he won't move a muscle, which we discover one night when we have to get a closer look.

"He's totally relaxed," Roger comments.

"And he has his buddy, Rex, with him," I add. The images of Rex's face on the pillow and blanket, still covering the sofa, surround him with love.

One day that summer when the sun is bright and high in the sky, I sit on a lounge chair outside. The sun warms my bare shoulders while the flicker of a cool wind whisks across my skin. The memories of many years here in this backyard with Rex seem to flash by. The warmth of love and happiness for all the time we had together now mingles with the chill of loss. I miss him so much and realize nothing will ever replace his sweet face, his tender eyes, and the touch of his cold nose.

Off to the side of the yard we have a Comet, a four-person, two-seater swing with a covered canopy. We bought it at a closeout sale and replaced the fabric with a striped pattern of forest green, tan, and white. We enjoy having friends over to join us on the swing; we enjoy tall, cool drinks while we push with our feet to make the swing move. Its shaded aluminum floor was Rex's favorite place to escape the summer heat. Charlie has never set foot on it.

When I look up from a book I'm reading, I see Charlie in the center of the swing, lying prone with his head on his paws, like Rex used to do.

I sniffle back a tear, and when Roger comes out to join me, I point to his little boy.

"Charlie is channeling his inner Rex," I say.

"Well, look at that. Rex loved that spot."

"He did, didn't he?"

We look at each other and smile.

Chapter Thirty-Three

THE FIRST OF THE month is weigh-in day. I'm on a personal kick to eat better; three years ago, I found myself out of breath when I climbed two flights of stairs. And then, on a moderate hike with my grandsons, my heart started pounding heavily.

"Your blood pressure is too high," my doctor said. "You need to bring that down."

Heart disease runs in the females in my family. My mom, her sister, and their mother were all affected. Feeling winded after mild exertion was a warning sign.

"You're not that overweight," she continued, "but if you lost fifteen to twenty pounds, it would make a big difference."

With the words of my doctor ringing in my ears, I made changes in my eating habits. Three years later, I'm forty-five pounds lighter. It isn't easy, but staying healthy is important. Roger joins me in trying to eat more healthily so he won't gain weight after quitting smoking.

I look at Charlie Bear. Rex had trouble for a few years when he put on some pounds, and I thought it might have contributed to his problems with his joints. I worked hard to get the weight off of Rex; and we did it, getting him down to a trim seventy-five pounds when he was around nine or ten.

I think it's as important to help Charlie Bear keep his trim, healthy shape, maybe even more so because he's small. I don't want him to become a roly-poly, little butterball.

Right now he fits perfectly on the arm of Roger's recliner. If he were any bigger, he'd fall off. So I tell Charlie the story of "Goldilocks and the Three Bears." I talk about how Papa Bear's bed is too hard, Mama Bear's bed is too soft, but Baby Bear's bed is *just right.* "That's you and the arm on Papa's chair, Charlie Bear. It's exactly your size."

When he first came to us, he weighed almost eighteen pounds. Well-meaning friends, and even Roger, showed Charlie their affection by offering him pieces of food or several doggie treats. I understand the intention. If one piece is good, two pieces are better—but not in this case.

I look up the recommended amount of food I should be feeding a dog his size and use a measuring cup for accuracy. For the first few days, Charlie gobbles up his food, looks at his empty bowl, and then stares up at me.

"You've had enough, little guy," I say. Cutting down on his snacks is easy. We don't cut them out entirely, but instead of two or three, we give him only one. By adhering to our commitment, Charlie drops a pound.

"Today is weigh-in day, Charlie Bear," I sing out to him and carry the glass-and-chrome scale into the kitchen. I have a goal weight I like to maintain, and I want Charlie to maintain a healthy weight too. He loves food like I do, but for the sake of our health, we have to be vigilant. Moderation is my motto.

I weigh myself first. After the number pops up on the digital readout, I make a note of it.

"Your turn, Charlie Bear." I scoop him into my arms and step onto the scale. "Okay, let's see what we get."

Along with watching what we eat, it's important to exercise. We have our routine walks, but those times when we play fetch in the yard or the chase-and-grab game in the house are also important. And when we can, we take Charlie for a swim. He's used to swimming now. I think he likes it, because the last time we went in the pool, he leapt off the step and swam like a little fish.

All this helps to keep Charlie trim. "So, what's your weight today?" I look at the first number subtracted from the second and grin.

"Sixteen pounds, Charlie Bear. That's great. Last month you were sixteen and a half, so you're down to where you should be."

I don't get concerned about half a pound up or down for either Charlie Bear or me, but if he balloons up to eighteen or nineteen in a month, that's when I'll be uneasy.

I take the scale upstairs and then join Charlie in the family room. I toss him the green banana.

Something is happening to me and to my feelings for this dog. I don't quite have a handle on it yet, but just as Roger quits smoking and takes control of his health, I want this little munchkin to have a long, healthy life.

Chapter Thirty-Four

I DID A LOT with Rex, but we never took him along to hotels with us. We could have found locations that accepted dogs of his size, but we never even considered it because he had Nancy, his doggie day care provider. When he was young and full of vim and vigor, she took him in at her place whenever we went away. It was the perfect solution. We went away for a good time, and Rex went to her place for a grand time. He was often more pooped when he came home than we were.

When he didn't have the stamina to play hard for a string of days, we called Emily.

Now, when I consider the fact that Charlie Bear is small, house-trained, and doesn't bark too much, I think he might possibly join us on our excursions.

We have an overnight outing coming up in August, which will combine business and pleasure. It could be an experiment to see how Charlie works out. I check the hotels in the area, and for a small fee, one will accept dogs that are under twenty-five pounds.

"Hon, should we bring Charlie Bear with us on our trip?" I ask a few weeks before we're scheduled to go.

"That might be fun. I'll be gone for almost the entire day, and you'd have Charlie with you to pass the time. Check it out."

"I already did. He can come."

We're going to Lake Arrowhead, a sleepy, small, picturesque town up in the San Bernardino Mountains. It's filled with quaint shops, mom-and-pop restaurants, and a crystal blue lake filled with fresh, clean runoff from the snow-capped mountains.

It's about two hours north and east of our home, and it's a pretty drive to get there. The winding road takes you higher and higher, up over five thousand feet, until you're above the clouds. When I can steal a peek out of the car window, I see the valley spread out before me. The clouds look like a blanket, thick and white, that blocks out cities, businesses, cars, and people.

Part of the ride includes wiggly, curvy, switchback roads—the only way to gain the necessary elevation to get up to Lake Arrowhead. I have a hard time with motion sickness, so I take an over-the-counter pill the morning we leave.

I should have kept my eyes looking out toward the car's front window, but I turn around a lot from the front seat to check on Charlie Bear. At first, he puts his paws on the armrest and sticks his nose up to catch the breeze from the partly lowered window.

Later, he paces the backseat, walking from one side to the other.

"Charlie, lie down," I urge.

"Is he okay?" Roger asks, his eyes on the road. "We're going to start climbing now, lots of twists and turns."

"He's okay." But about halfway up the last section of the mountain, a few miles shy of our destination, Charlie begins to turn a little green. His face has a tell-tale look, like he's trying to hold something in.

Then it happens.

"Stop the car. Pull over."

"Why, what's wrong?"

"Charlie threw up."

I can't blame him, I want to throw up too. Animals often get motion sickness for the same reason people do.

Roger slides the SUV onto a gravel-filled spot off the main road. I grab some napkins from the glove compartment and a plastic bag.

"Charlie Bear," Roger says with deep concern. "Are you okay?"

"He's okay. He wants the car to stop." I don't add I want it to as well.

"We're almost to the hotel. Can he hang on a little longer?"

"He'll be fine." I tie the bag shut and tuck it under the seat, and then I pat Charlie's head. "Poor Charlie, I understand how you feel."

Finally, Roger pulls into the hotel parking lot. We walk Charlie into the lobby with his black leash attached to his bright red collar.

"He is so cute," the receptionist at the front desk exclaims. "What kind of dog is he?"

"We're not sure. A Heinz 57 maybe?" I smile, and she hands me the paperwork to sign. To Roger, she slides a placard across the counter that reads, "Dog on the loose."

"Hang this on the outside of the door to your room. If you're not there, housekeeping will not enter and inadvertently let your dog out."

We're handed a key for a room on the first floor. Charlie Bear smells dogs all over the place. He sniffs his way down the hallway and all over the room when we step inside. He checks out the baseboards, the sofa, the bathroom, and the little balcony, which has a high wall all the way around it. The room has a big bed, a small TV, a couch, an ottoman, a desk, and a chair.

I bring out his water and food and encourage Charlie to consume both. He laps up some water and denies the food, but he does appear to have his bearings back.

What he does next is classic, high-spirited Charlie. He jumps, leaps, and dives from the bed to the ottoman to the sofa.

"He bounces back quickly from being sick," Roger notes.

"Literally."

CHAPTER THIRTY-FIVE

WE SET CHARLIE BEAR up with his own bed that we bring from home, the rounded fleece one, and put it on the sofa with a blanket underneath. The first night is a trial for all of us.

Charlie doesn't want to sleep in his bed. I knew this would happen. He'd rarely slept in his crate lately at home, so we didn't bring it, and now, without a crate to confine him, Charlie has the freedom of the entire room. It's silly of me to think he'll go over to his fleece bed and curl up for the night when his papa is a few feet away. He jumps onto our bed and sleeps there, alternating between curling up in Roger's arms and spreading out between us.

The next day, Roger leaves to attend his meeting; he'll be gone almost ten hours. After a leisurely cup of coffee and a serene morning of responding to e-mails and catching up on Facebook, I look at the clock. It's almost noon.

"Want to go for a walk, Charlie?"

We head out for a lengthy stroll along the lake. I tie a long, yellow nylon rope to his collar so he can sprint ahead of me down the path and then race back. He doesn't have our backyard to run in, but he still needs his Indy 500 time to diffuse his doggy energy.

Maybe it's the altitude, but Charlie pants a bit about halfway through our walk. I pull out his water bottle, and we stop often. We take up a perch on a bench to watch boats zoom across the sparkling lake.

Water-skiers entertain us by flying off the ends of their towropes when they hit a rogue wave. Then they excite us with their efforts as they try again and again to rise up from the cold, blue water. "Woo hoo," they yell when they master the skill of balancing on two narrow boards while being pulled behind a speeding boat. It's fun to watch them because I've done it, and it's not easy. I applaud their determination.

We head to our room at about three o'clock and snooze a little on the sofa. My cell phone rings late in the afternoon. Roger is on his way back. Charlie and I walk out to the parking lot to meet him.

"Charlie Bear, did you have a good day?" Roger asks and takes the end of the rope from my hands.

"We had a great day. The lake is so pretty in August."

"After we take Charlie Bear inside, do you want to walk over to the shops and get some pizza?"

"I'd love to."

The quaint pizza joint has a few tables inside and a large, wooden deck outside, overlooking the lake. Tall flagpoles line the entire area, and the evening breeze breathes life into the red-and-white flags surrounding us. A three-piece band plays catchy tunes in the corner, while a large group celebrates a young girl's birthday.

We walk up to the window. They have an extensive menu of salads, pizza combinations and sandwiches. We order two small pizzas and a large salad to share. Roger picks pepperoni for his pizza, and I choose a Hawaiian, with pineapple and green pepper instead of ham.

We sit outside for a while and brave the cooling temperature.

"Are you cold?" Roger asks.

"A little," I respond and pull my light jacket closer around me.

"Let's go inside." Roger gathers our napkins, plates, and pizzas, and I bring our drinks.

"Better?"

"Much better," I respond, and we finish our meal.

I'm grateful for this little getaway together. It's been nice. We hold hands and swing them between us on the walk back.

"I have a surprise for you," I say.

"What's that?"

"Wait and see."

Back in the room, I dig out two small paper plates, two forks, and a knife from a bag stashed in the bottom of our luggage. I hid a small chocolate cake in the room's tiny refrigerator, and now I stick a large candle on it, light it, and walk out from the bathroom singing,

Happy anniversary to you.

Happy anniversary to you.

Happy anniversary, dear Roger.

And many, many more.

Roger beams from where he sits, lounging on the sofa with Charlie at his side.

"Here Charlie, I have something for you." I scatter a bacon-flavored treat, broken into tiny pieces, around the floor and tell him to "find it."

I hand Roger the cake and kiss him on the cheek. "You've made it one entire year. I am so proud of you."

"Thanks. This is nice of you."

"You deserve it. Blow out your candle, and make a wish."

Three-hundred and sixty-five days without a cigarette—quite an accomplishment.

I slice a piece of cake for both of us.

"This is sweet," Roger comments while we eat.

"It is pretty sugary."

"I mean it's sweet of you to buy me a cake."

By this time, Charlie has finished with his treats and climbs up into Roger's lap.

"A couple more months and he'll have been with us for a year." I'm already thinking about a little celebration.

"Wow, time rushes by. Doesn't it?"

"Sure does."

I put the rest of the cake into the box and stick it in the refrigerator. "Don't let me forget to bring it home tomorrow."

Later, I take Charlie Bear outside on his leash through a side door. I did the same thing last night, but on this evening, there's a big, black Lab hanging around right outside the door. He doesn't have a leash on. In fact, he's holding his folded leash in his teeth while he prances in the grass. A man sits on the curb a few feet away.

The dog spots us and begins to walk our way. Charlie barks and lunges on his leash. I lift him off the ground and into my arms. The man calls his dog, but by then Charlie is fixated on the Lab and barks furiously while I hold him. I carry Charlie off and whisper in his ear to be quiet, but I can't blame him. The rules at this hotel explicitly state all dogs are to be on leash at all times. The rules are the rules for a good reason. I wish this man and his dog hadn't broken them.

We walk toward the end of the parking lot and stop at a grassy area where I put Charlie Bear down. After a few minutes, we head inside; the man and his dog are now gone from near the door.

In the room, Charlie exuberantly tackles Roger on the bed, but this time his playing doesn't last long. He's tired and melts into the comforter next to Roger's chest.

I look at the two of them. Roger finally has the warmth and devotion of a snuggly dog to cuddle and sleep with. This is what he wanted all those months ago, and it looks like this plucky little dog wants the same thing too.

In the morning, it's time to head home. Roger chooses a route that's a bit gentler on the queasy stomachs of his riders. I thank him with abundance, even if it does take longer to get home.

We pull into the driveway and unload the car.

"Charlie, I'm super proud of you." He's on Roger's lap, stretched out like usual, the two of them relaxing and watching TV. "You didn't lift your leg even one time inside the hallways, in the lobby, in the room, or on the patio. Not even once."

"That's right, Charlie Bear. You were perfect," Roger adds.

"If he behaved so well this time, maybe we'll be able to take him on a road trip again?"

"Maybe, we'll see."

"There's one thing Charlie wants you to think about, though." I cross my arms over my chest, tilt my head to the side, and stare at Roger.

"What's that?"

"He doesn't like wiggly, curvy, switchback roads."

Roger scratches behind Charlie's ears. "You don't like wiggle roads, huh?"

"He'd rather be on the straight and narrow."

"That's how we'd both like you to be, Charlie Bear, on a straight and narrow path. Do you think you can do that?"

Charlie flicks his tongue out for a quick kiss.

I smile at them. "We'll see. His one-year anniversary is two months away."

Maybe it's the altitude. After all, at more than five thousand feet, we're pretty close to heaven. Or maybe it's something else. But on that second night in Lake Arrowhead, I have a dream. And it's very vivid.

I see the big dog, and he tells me about what happens when he goes over the rainbow bridge.

Here's what Rex says:

When I get here, there's a long line. Dogs, cats, raccoons, possums, you name it. Time passes, though. We all talk to each other, and soon enough the black mastiff with the clipboard calls out, "Next."

I trot up.

"Name?"

"Rex Taylor."

"Age?"

"Going on twelve."

"Family here?"

"Uh, lots. Diamond, Red, Pickles, Pepper, Bandit—" but he cuts me off.

"Just immediate family please."

"Diamond and Red."

The head of intake jots a note on his clipboard and then presses the button on his walkie-talkie. "Rex Taylor is here. Send up Diamond and Red."

A crackle emanates from the small black box. "They're already on their way. They knew he was coming."

"Ten-four," Intake says. "Last question. Who did you leave behind?"

"Mom and Dad, B.J. and Roger Taylor, and a scruffy mutt named Charlie Bear."

He notes that on his clipboard as well. "Okay, Rex, go on in. Rainbow bridge is straight ahead. You'll find your friends on the other side."

"Thanks." I run the short distance toward the brilliant light. It's crazy pretty here. Lots of flowers, birds, butterflies, and trees. My legs are strong now, no hitch or limp at all. I'm back up to my seventy-five pounds of muscle, and the gray hair on my face is replaced by a golden brown, like when I was young.

The bridge is wooden, and my nails make a clickity, click sound as I scamper over. And then there they are.

Red has filled back out and no longer has mats of fur plastered to his body. His marmalade color shines in the sun.

I walk over and lick him like I always used to. He sidles up to me and rubs against my leg.

And then there's Diamond. Her pretty gray-and-white face and statuesque body perch near us, but far enough away to be safe. She eyes me with those bright green eyes of hers and seems to say, "Welcome." I acknowledge her with a nod.

Red leads the way into the valley toward a huge lake. "And there's a beach just over the hill. We know how you love to run in the sand."

I stop for a drink of water and then bring my head up and look around. This place is beautiful, and it's where I'll be waiting for my family members when they arrive.

I don't know about you, but I want to go there. Not soon, mind you, but it sounds fantastic.

The next time Mom sits in her office and stares out the window, I mosey my way over to her and wiggle my tail. She picks me up and holds me on her lap. Soon, I feel her body heave with sobs, and wet drops fall onto my fur. I crane my neck around and lick her face. We sit that way, together, for a long time.

CHAPTER THIRTY-SIX

THE END OF AUGUST is a special day for Charlie Bear. It's his birthday, and he turns two.

"Oh no," I said to Roger a few days before Charlie's big day on the twenty-eighth. "He's going into the terrible twos, like a toddler."

Roger laughs. "It can't be much worse than the way he's been already, can it?"

"I sure hope not."

I think about Charlie's short life history. For most dogs, and for people, too, a birthday is just another day, but Ryo and Sara both thought Charlie might not make it to two years old. By this age, most dogs have become part of the family. Not Charlie Bear. He still struggled with feeling comfortable in his surroundings.

A vet determined Charlie's age was right under a year when Sara first took him in. He lived with her for four months, and then he came to live with us.

"We need to celebrate his big day," I tell Roger after work that night.

After dinner, I bring out two little slices of cheesecake, with a lit candle in each one, and we sing "Happy Birthday" to Charlie.

Our singing is pretty bad, but I give us a B+ for effort.

We blow out the candles for Charlie and then eat the pieces of cake ourselves. "No cheesecake for you, Charlie, but here's a yummy chicken treat."

He gobbles that up, and then we tell him we have something else.

"Charlie, here's a present for you."

Roger pulls a brand-new toy out of a paper sack. It's a stuffed gray kitty cat with golden eyes, white paws, a pink nose, and a set of white whiskers. He sets it down on the carpet. Charlie grabs it and then runs to the sofa with the cat in his mouth.

"He likes it," Roger says.

At the end of the day—a day some people speculated Charlie would never reach—he's tuckered out, so he does what he likes to do best. He jumps onto the sofa in his room, sticks his four white feet into the air, and hangs his head down over the end.

Happy Birthday, Charlie.

CHAPTER THIRTY-SEVEN

THE SECOND WEEK IN September, Roger and I have another trip to take. We've never been to Sedona, Arizona, the place where massive, red rock formations spring from the valley floor in an awesome display of color and size. We've seen the photographs that beautifully depict these red rocks, and we want to see them and experience the spiritual essence of this majestic place.

We've been planning this trip since the spring, when our friends in Arizona asked us to meet them there, but Charlie can't come along. We'll be staying at a hotel that doesn't allow pets, and on top of that, we'll be shopping, dining out, and playing golf. We'll be gone from our room most of the day, and it wouldn't be fair, even if we were in a pet-friendly hotel, to leave Charlie Bear alone for such long stretches of time in a strange place.

Roger and I debate what would be best for Charlie. Should we ask Sara to take him in for those five days and nights? We can, but he might get confused. This is where he lives, and we don't want to mix him up. That might send him into a tailspin, and we don't want more of that.

Dr. Love's veterinary office provides boarding and care, and in a pinch, we can always take him there. But if at all possible, we want to keep him in his routine with the least amount of stress.

Another option is to have someone come and stay at our home with Charlie, but we don't know anyone who does that. And he isn't like Rex, who used to go to Nancy's doggie day care and board overnight when we were on vacation. Charlie won't fit in there with all the large dogs.

"So what do we do?" Roger asks one evening when we're discussing our choices.

"Why don't we call in Emily? She's always done a fabulous job for us."

"She gave Red his insulin shots. But other than that, Red and Diamond didn't need much except for food, water, and litter-box cleaning. And Rex was older and slept most of the day."

I look at Roger as he speaks. His face tightens with concern when he adds, "Charlie is so young. He needs more than that."

"Emily will come over and play with him, and she'll be sure he goes to bed at night in his room. He'll sleep in his own bed, run around his own house, watch his backyard for possums, and play with his own toys. And after she gets him up in the morning and feeds him, she can give him his Kong with peanut butter when she leaves."

"I don't know," Roger adds. "Will Emily's two visits a day be enough?"

"I think so, but if you want more activity going on in the house, why not ask the kids to come by and spend some time with him?" Our grown daughter and son both live within thirty miles of our house. "They'll be the perfect mix of companionship, care, and love."

"I'll call and see if they can fit it into their schedules."

Before we leave, Roger has it all worked out. Emily will come by twice a day, and our daughter will check on Charlie every other night. Our son will stop by in the afternoons.

"Charlie, be a good boy while we're gone." Roger snuggles him extra tight.

It's a seven-hour ride to Sedona. We're on the I-10 freeway for most of the drive, and then we head north out of Phoenix on I-17. When we finally turn off onto the Sedona exit, I'm a bit disappointed. All I see is scrub and brush and low-lying mountains—the same scenery I've seen out my window for most of the long drive.

We come around a curve in the road and *bam*, the massive formations are breathtaking. This truly is Red Rock Country, as it is called. The formations spring up from the floor of the canyon and thrust toward the heavens, each crop of rock more stunning and more intensely red than the next.

We find our hotel at the beginning of town, but we don't turn in. We keep driving for a while, getting the lay of the land and inhaling the beauty of this majestic place. When we finally drive back to the hotel and check in, we find an incredible view from the balcony of our room. We unpack the car and get settled; then we go over to the pool for a swim.

"Let's talk about what we're going to do for the next few days," Roger says.

We pick up a vacation planner, compliments of the hotel, and look at the many places to visit.

"There's something called Fiesta Del Tlaquepaque going on this weekend," I say as we pore over the material. "That sounds like fun. There will be music and food. It's in the Tlaquepaque Arts and Crafts Village."

"Here it is on the map," Roger adds.

"Can we do some shopping uptown? The check-in clerk said the stores are fabulous there."

"Sure."

We take note of the many restaurants, everything from gourmet pizza to a Mexican restaurant called Javelina Cantina. We plan a few activities, leaving plenty of time for spontaneity.

I look around at the mountains and then over at Roger. "I wish Charlie Bear were here. He'd like this pool."

"When we get back to the room, let's check in on him," Roger says.

That night we call Emily. "How's Charlie doing?"

"Oh, he's so sweet, and he's totally glad to see me. He wiggles and wags that cute little body of his. After he ate and we played, I tossed small pieces of treats around his room when I put him to bed. I turned on his nightlight and put up the barrier across the doorway like you said to do in your note of instructions."

"So no messes in the house—nothing chewed up?" I ask.

"Nope. He was a good boy."

"You have our cell phone numbers. Call if anything at all comes up, okay?"

"You bet. He's fine. I'm taking good care of him."

The next night our daughter sends a text photo to Roger's cell phone with the message: *I miss you.* We both laugh at the speed of technology. Who would think two older people on vacation hundreds of miles away could be reassured their beloved pet is fine at home?

Our daughter later snuggles with Charlie in Roger's chair, holds him close, and whispers to him softly.

"He even falls asleep in my arms. He is so cute," her text says two days later.

We swim in the hotel pool, share drinks with our friends on the balcony of our room, play golf on two nearby courses, and go to dinner at a fine restaurant called Cucina Rustica with an authentic Italian atmosphere. Roger and I enjoy lunch on our own at Javelina Cantina the day before our friends arrive, and then end up back at that same restaurant with them. We don't mind one bit, the food is fantastic; the warm tortilla chips and fresh salsa are a big hit.

The shops are filled with kitschy collectibles, and we bring home our fair share. We even splurge on a one-foot-tall portable fan for my desk at the office. It's made of metal and is in the shape of a dog with long, floppy, caramel-colored ears like Rex's. In his left paw, he holds a golf club.

We snap tons of pictures of the beautiful red rock, the classic formations very similar to those in the Grand Canyon. We even visit the Holy Cross Chapel up high on a hill with a stunning view of the valley. We light a candle inside and place a dollar into the donation cup. Then we say our prayers for good health and safe travels.

We wake up on our last morning and hit the road almost before the sun comes up. By early afternoon, we're home.

"Charlie Bear," Roger exclaims with excitement when we open the door. "Did you miss us?"

Charlie bounces across the room. His whole body shakes and wiggles with happiness.

Roger sits in his recliner and is accosted with the most licks and kisses Charlie has ever doled out.

"I missed you too," Roger says, smiling a big, broad grin, which tells me he is extra thrilled to be home with his beloved dog in his arms.

CHAPTER THIRTY-EIGHT

THE MONTH OF SEPTEMBER flies by, and before you can snap your fingers, October is back. With it comes cooler weather, the promise of fall on the horizon, and holidays that are again around the corner.

One year ago this month, Charlie came to be with us.

I know the date exactly. Milestone dates etch themselves into my memory. If you ask me about an important event, I can tell you on what date it occurred—Roger's birthday, our anniversary, the dates the grandkids were born, the dates Diamond and Red left us, the date Rex went over the rainbow bridge, the date my dad died, the date my mom passed right before Christmas.

I know every important date. And this one is no different.

October 16.

A year ago, we began the search for a tiny Yorkie, a small, lively dog to join our household and to ease the emptiness of Red's passing. Instead of a Yorkie, we fall for a slightly larger dog, one full of attitude, spunk, and headstrong will. The past year has been a challenge in many ways. Roger struggles through the changes that occur in his body after he quits smoking, and I lose my mom and Rex.

In one of the many magazines crammed inside my mailbox at this time of year, I discover two precious Christmas ornaments. I buy them and tuck them away in the hall cupboard. They're pewter medallion picture frames (one for a female and one for a male) with a circle of red hearts around the center. I insert a photograph of Rex in one and of Mom in the other. At the top of the ornament, a bright red bow is inscribed with the words, "In loving memory." Around the perimeter of the ornament, these words form a ring:

God saw him getting tired,
a cure not meant to be,
so He wrapped His arms around him,
and whispered, "Come with Me."

Through everything that happens in the past year, day in and day out, there is Charlie Bear, the obstinate, bullheaded little monkey that somehow licks his way into our hearts.

A lot happens in a year.

Life changes.

Love takes hold.

And you think about your second chances.

Second chances—I've been given more than my fair share of them. I must admit, I rebelled and resisted. I've been obstinate and stubborn and filled with angst. Hey, wouldn't you be if you were abandoned on the streets as a pup and had to fend for yourself? Then when someone found you and gave you love, you didn't believe it could be real. Heck, the family you trusted sent you packing. What's to keep this person from doing the same?

So I get it in my head I'm not lovable. I'm a mess, that's for sure. An insecure, tough-on-the-outside-but-tender-on-the-inside mess of a mutt. It takes special people to see beyond my exterior shell.

Dad sees it right away. He melts my hard and tough posture, and I become a liquid, moldable puppy in his arms. But old habits are hard to release. I want to let them go, I really do, but it takes a long time.

And time is what they give me. Time is what I give Mom too. She doesn't love me the way Dad loves me. She can't see past the hard outer shell like Dad does. And she doesn't think she'll survive another heartbreak, like the one she experienced when Red passed away right before I got here. She can't give in to loving me. She wants to, but it's hard for her.

We're struggling, me and Mom. We've been through a tough time. We're both battling these demons of mistrust and lack of faith. I don't blame her, not one bit.

When the big dog dies, something dies with Mom. When she takes Rex on his journey over the rainbow bridge, a piece of her heart breaks off and goes with him and never comes back. She says she has a hole in her heart. Whatever you call it, it's real. It's life. It's what happens in this world.

When my first people send me out of their home, I lose a piece of my heart too. I trusted them. I loved them. I thought we'd be together forever.

Now I'm learning to trust again, to love again, to believe in the future.

It has been a whole year now. An entire year with these new peeps whom I have come to love (even Mom because I can see into her heart, and I know what's in there).

I still have some things to work on. I think all rescue dogs come with memories of their pasts that creep up on them once in a while, like PTSD takes hold of a soldier.

Therapy. Training. Patience. Love. Those are the remedies. Oh, and there's also a big one I forgot. Time. It takes time, lots of time, to layer new memories over old, to place good feelings over bad ones. Mom talks about the "firsts" you go through when grieving. That's a good thing for me to remember. I had to go through that as well when I was welcomed into my new home.

I'm thankful for the second chances I've been given in my short two years of life. If I could go back, I'd change some of the things I've done, but I can't go back. I can only go forward.

So I'm moving into the future one day at a time. I'm giving Dad the abundance of love he gives back to me and reaching out a little more toward Mom each day.

We've got time. And we have more second chances.

Chapter Thirty-Nine

It's my birthday only days after Charlie's anniversary, and I think about the past fifty years of my life—the ups, the downs, the loves, and the losses.

Moments of missing Mom, and Dad too, surge through me at times. A song plays on the radio, a memory bursts into my mind, and it's bittersweet to remember them both. I think of them often and imagine them up in heaven together. It's comforting to think of them watching over me, encouraging me, and supporting me.

Months after losing Rex, I still sob and still miss him so badly. I fill out a prayer card that comes from the Best Friends Animal Society in Kanab, Utah. They have a beautiful place there, a haven for dogs, cats, horses and other animals that need temporary or permanent homes. I fill out the card, my hand shaking, "Please remember Rex at the Angels Rest Blessing." There's a spot for a photograph, so I clip one down to size and paste it on. Then I write next to it, "Rex—such a good boy, with a heart of gold."

More tears—so many tears. Will the pain ever go away? I want to see him, hold him, touch him, and hug him. I long for his compassionate eyes, his sweet face, and his gentle nature. His nuzzles into my neck, his full-body warmth at my side. I still have his pink scrap of a blanket, his collar and leash, and his food bowls marked with his name on them. I still hear his deep "woof" greeting me when I pull into the garage. I still see him standing on the other side of the gate, his tail wagging a welcome.

Months later, I still miss him.

My sobs bring Charlie Bear swishing into the room. He jumps onto the sofa and looks at me with intense, dark eyes. I want to love him fully, I do, but that would mean opening myself up to hurt again, and my heart is already torn open and raw.

Wouldn't it be better to protect myself from this type of pain? Wouldn't it be wise to close myself off? I can't let myself love this little guy, not like that, not completely. It will hurt too much in the end.

I look over at Charlie's sweet face. There's something about him. I want to fight it, but it floods through me like a river overflowing its banks, and I discover this emotion has been there all along.

It has been there from the moment I laid eyes on his picture to the day he first appeared at our door and snuggled onto my husband's lap, peppering Roger with little kisses.

I loved him from the beginning.

It's true, there will never be another dog for me like Rex. He was a loving, mellow soul and truly one of a kind, and we shared a deep bond together. But that doesn't mean I can't love another. Haven't I already given my heart to many dogs and cats over the years? Haven't I lived through the heartache and pain over and over again?

Maybe this past year hit me extra hard because of how many losses there were. Maybe I need to pray for more strength, more faith, more trust.

More time.

Charlie wiggles his body and inclines his head forward. I bend toward him and kiss his neck. He jumps down from the sofa and leaves the room.

Sure, he's Roger's dog through and through, and Roger has given him the love and compassion he needed for the past year. But the more I open up my heart to love Charlie Bear, the more love he'll give back to me.

I take in a deep breath and then whisper the words: "Rex, I miss you. I know you're fine in heaven. Be at peace, sweetheart. I'll always love you."

I get up. There'll be days when the tears will still come, but that's okay.

I'm ready now for life, love, and second chances.

Just this side of heaven is a place called rainbow bridge.

*When an animal dies that has been
especially close to someone here,*

that pet goes to rainbow bridge.

There are meadows and hills for all of our special friends,

*so they can run and play together. There is plenty of food,
water, and sunshine,*

and our friends are warm and comfortable.

*All the animals who had been ill and old
are restored to health and vigor;*

*those who were hurt or maimed are
made whole and strong again,*

*just as we remember them in our dreams
of days and times gone by.*

The animals are happy and content, except for one small thing;

*they each miss someone very special to
them, who had to be left behind.*

They all run and play together, but the day comes

when one suddenly stops and looks into the distance.

His bright eyes are intent; his eager body quivers.

*Suddenly, he begins to run from the
group, flying over the green grass,*

his legs carrying him faster and faster.

*You have been spotted, and when you and
your special friend finally meet,*

you cling together in joyous reunion, never to be parted again.

*The happy kisses rain upon your face; your
hands again caress the beloved head,*

and you look once more into the trusting eyes of your pet,

so long gone from your life but never absent from your heart.

Then you cross rainbow bridge together.

* * *

Author Unknown

Charlie Bear in Crate

Charlie Bear
Ever Watchful on
Recliner Arm

Charlie Bear with
B.J. at Pool

Charlie Bear
with Attitude

Diamond
and Red

Puppy Rex

Rex on His Sofa

Rex with B.J. at Beach

Rex at 11

ACKNOWLEDGMENTS

I DIDN'T GO LOOKING for this story. It found me. Charlie Bear plunged into my life in a big way, and his was a story begging to be told. Without the help of Ryoko Matsui, his rescuer, and Sara Golden, his foster mom, Charlie would not have been up for adoption. Now, he is a huge part of my life.

I'd like to thank all of the many people who, like Ryo and Sara, work diligently 24–7 for the cause of "No More Homeless Pets." As a huge supporter of the Best Friends Animal Society, I believe we can someday make that happen. It all begins with looking at shelters and rescue sites and taking a chance on a dog that needs a forever home.

Special thanks to all of the people at Inspiring Voices for helping me tell Charlie Bear's story. The editors at *Guideposts* magazine have been amazing. And I don't know where I'd be without my wonderful agent, Jonathan Clements. Thank you for believing in me.

The roots of my writing world travel all the way back to 1996, and I would be remiss if I didn't mention my talented mentors, Kay Marshall Strom and Dan Kline, who nurtured the seedling of a writer during those Saturday morning classes at California State University, Long Beach. A fledgling writers group was born shortly thereafter. I owe a debt of gratitude to the Sixteen Thumbs for their patience, helpfulness, and focused feedback: Jean Stewart, Sallie Rodman, Linda Frankel, Dierdre Zane, Julie Sanford, Tsgoyna Tanzman, and Theresa Theiler. A swift kick in the keister came from a good writer friend, Merrie Destefano, who made me prioritize my work these past few years and buckle in for the long haul. And with her positive, cheerleading smile, Andrea Verde kept me reaching for more. And then there are the Marble Shapers, a group of inspiring *Guideposts* writers who beckon me onward from all across the United States: Julie Garmon, Peggy Frezon, Susan Karas, Wanda Rosseland, Stephanie Thompson, Catherine Madera, and Mary Lou Reed.

My life has been enriched in multiple ways by the adoption of Charlie Bear. If it weren't for the instant love and attraction between my husband and Charlie Bear, he wouldn't have joined our lives. Roger, my devotion to you probably doesn't equal Charlie Bear's, but thank you for giving me the support and encouragement I needed to push forward.

With love,

B.J.

About the Author

B. J. Taylor is the author of *Sunny Side Up: Inspiring Stories for Dog & Cat Lovers; Sunny Side Up: Inspiring Stories for Tough Times;* and *Sunny Side Up: Inspiring Stories for Women.* B.J. believes that behind the clouds there is always the sun, and she offers up-close and personal stories that provide you with encouragement and hope.

B.J. inspires thousands of readers through her writing for *Guideposts* magazine, *Chicken Soup for the Soul,* and her well-known blog, Taylor's Tips. She is an award-winning author who enjoys connecting with readers through Facebook, her website, or through her blog, where Charlie Bear posts many of his thoughts on life. B.J., her husband, and their rescue dog, Charlie Bear, live in Southern California.

www.bjtayloronline.com

www.bjtaylorblog.wordpress.com

For More Information

In B.J.'s book *Sunny Side Up: Inspiring Stories for Dog & Cat Lovers,* you will find a bonus section devoted to Charlie Bear's life before adoption. It's the beginning of his story, told in short vignettes from Charlie Bear himself.

For more in Charlie's own words, go to Taylor's Tips Blog at www.bjtaylorblog.wordpress.com and click on the category "Charlie Chat." Charlie shares more of his thoughts on life before and after adoption, adjustment to his forever home, and now that he's turned two, ruminations on what he's learned. He's calling the new posts Y2K (Year 2 Know-it-all).

www.adoptapet.com
Find a dog, cat, or other animal to adopt, and search by breed, size, age and location.
Find a shelter or rescue group.

www.bestfriends.org
Best Friends Animal Society runs the nation's largest sanctuary for abused and abandoned animals. Their mission is to bring about a time when there are no more homeless pets.

Tales from Beyond: True Stories of Our Immortal Pets by Dr. Ann Redding & Ann Campbell

The Divine Life of Animals: One Man's Quest to Discover Whether the Souls of Animals Live On by Ptolemy Tompkins

Animals and the Afterlife: True Stories of Our Best Friends' Journey Beyond Death by Kim Sheridan

A NOTE FROM THE EDITORS

WE HOPE YOU ENJOY *Charlie Bear*, specially selected by the editors of the Books and Inspirational Media Division of Guideposts, a nonprofit organization. In all of our books, magazines and outreach efforts, we aim to deliver inspiration and encouragement, help you grow in your faith, and celebrate God's love in every aspect of your daily life.

Thank you for making a difference with your purchase of this book, which helps fund our many outreach programs to the military, prisons, hospitals, nursing homes and schools. To learn more, visit GuidepostsFoundation.org.

We also maintain many useful and uplifting online resources. Visit Guideposts.org to read true stories of hope and inspiration, access OurPrayer network, sign up for free newsletters, download free e-books, join our Facebook community, and follow our stimulating blogs.

To learn about other Guideposts publications, including our best-selling devotional *Daily Guideposts*, go to ShopGuideposts.org, call (800) 932-2145 or write to Guideposts, PO Box 5815, Harlan, Iowa 51593.